Turning The Tables:

THE STORY OF EXTREME CHAMPIONSHIP WRESTLING

By John Lister

British Library Cataloguing In Publication Data.
A Record of this Publication is available from the British Library.

ISBN 1905363788

First Published October 2005 by Exposure Publishing, an imprint of Diggory Press, Three Rivers, Minions, Liskeard, Cornwall PL14 5LE

WWW.DIGGORYPRESS.COM

Dedicated to the memory of Chris Candido, the last true worker.

Notes and acknowledgements

Directly-quoted source material is acknowledged throughout this book. More generally, this book simply would not have been possible without the work of the *Wrestling Observer*, *Pro Wrestling Torch*, and *Wrestling Lariat*. Other sources which proved particularly useful include David Fredericks' Philadelphia Wrestling Archive (**http://www.angelfire.com/sports/mrwrestling/**), the columns of Bob Magee (**www.pwbts.com**), Jason Campbell's **www.prowrestlinghistory.com**, and the legal research of Chad Smith and his colleagues at **www.otherarena.com**.

Special thanks are due to Mark Dunderdale, Kieran Lefort, Kenny McBride, Stuart Millard and Glen Radford for their help, advice and assistance.

North American readers should note this book uses British English spellings and customs wherever appropriate.

This book is not authorised or endorsed by World Wrestling Entertainment Inc. All cover photographs are the copyright of the author. The title typeface is Barbaric, produced by Aeryn's Foundry (**http://www.draftlight.net/aeryn/**) and used by kind permission.

While reasonable attempts have been made to verify all information in this book, the very nature of the professional wrestling business often makes the 'truth' little more than the more plausible of two contrasting exaggerations. If you would like to correct or clarify anything in this book, please e-mail **corrections@turningthetables.co.uk**. Any factual errors will be corrected at **www.turningthetables.co.uk**.

1: The city that booed Santa

"You can't book Philadelphia the way you book the rest of the country. It just can't be done." (Tod Gordon in a Pro Wrestling Torch *interview.)*

Philadelphia was different.

The title of 'The City of Brotherly Love' could only be used ironically when it came to Philadelphia sports. The Flyers hockey team was so renowned for its brawling style that its players were nicknamed the 'Broad Street Bullies'. And the Eagles football team had such rowdy fans that officials built a courtroom under the stadium to save time processing rioting fans. The team was forever known for a 1968 incident when 20-year-old Frank Olivo attempted to lift the crowd's spirits at half-time by dancing on the pitch dressed as Santa Claus; the home team fans responded with a round of boos before pelting him with snowballs.

Add this local flavour to the violent world of professional wrestling and you were guaranteed rowdy crowds. When Pedro Morales dropped the WWWF title to Stan Stasiak in 1972, the promotion dared not have a clear-cut result for genuine fear of a riot. Instead Morales landed a bridging suplex and Stasiak raised his shoulder; the ring announcer simply said "Let's hear it for a great champion, Pedro Morales", and fans did not get confirmation of the result until the following week's television.

After being built up before the war by promoter Ray Fabiani, Philadelphia was a key part of the WWWF territory (later WWF/WWE) right from the first time those initials were used in 1963. The Philadelphia Arena was home to the promotion's main television show, *Championship Wrestling*, as well as hosting live events until 1978. From 1974, the Philadelphia Spectrum was used for major monthly shows drawing up to 19,500 fans; in 1996 the promotion moved to the new First Union (now Wachovia) Center.

But from the mid-80s, Philadelphia wasn't just a WWF city: it was a wrestling city. Along with Baltimore, it was one of the first places where the Carolinas-based Jim Crockett Promotions (under the

NWA banner) countered Vince McMahon's own national expansion. Locked out of the Spectrum, Crockett promoted at the Philadelphia Civic Center and quickly built up crowds with what hardcore fans considered superior wrestling action. On the first head-to-head clash on 10 January 1987, Crockett achieved an 11,000 sellout; though the WWF's 14,000 crowd was bigger, Crockett's higher-priced tickets meant he drew the bigger gate. Either way, Philadelphia was clearly a hot town for wrestling: when the business hit a major collapse five years later, one cable company reported New Jersey and Philadelphia were the only markets where wrestling pay-per-views were still a guaranteed success.

But the most dedicated of the Philadelphia fans wanted more than the two national promotions had to offer. Local Prudential insurance worker Joel Goodhart tried everything he could think of to serve this need. He opened a wrestling store in 1985, promoted local events for the NWA, hosted a wrestling show on local radio, ran the Ringmasters training school, and launched the 'Squared Circle Fan Club', an organisation that took Philadelphia fans on bus trips as far afield as the Memphis territory and even persuaded the usually tight-lipped Jerry Lawler to address the hardcore fans at a Philadelphia banquet.

Come the turn of the decade, Goodhart took the next logical step and launched his own promotion, the Tri-State Wrestling Alliance, with the memorable slogan "We wrestle, we brawl, we do it all!" Violence was at the heart of the product, and in a 1991 interview with academic researcher Lee Benaka, Goodhart said he deliberately didn't market to children, estimating that 75% of his audience was over 30. He obviously felt this was a viable business model, claiming "I plan to be a millionaire in this business... I plan to make a substantial sum of money giving fans what they want."

If what they wanted was big names and chaotic action, they were happy. The likes of Terry Funk, Jerry Lawler, Abdullah the Butcher, Kerry Von Erich, Paul Orndorff and Rick Rude headlined the promotion's quarterly 'supershows' at Pennsylvania Hall (a smaller building in the Civic Center complex), while local wrestlers such as Mr Sandman, DC Drake, Larry Winters and JT Smith continued the bloody action on around 40 smaller shows a year. Among the less conventional matches on offer were an audience participation lumberjack match, a reverse steel cage battle royal (where the wrestlers started on the floor and the last man inside the cage won), and an infamous best-of-three series between Cactus Jack and Eddie Gilbert where the first match had falls count anywhere, the second stretcher rules, and the third was a cage match. Even the future 'hardcore legend' Cactus thought things might be overdone; writing in his autobiography *Have A Nice Day* he said "Joel's shows were the circus equivalent of seeing a guy get shot out of a cannon thirty times. On small shows, in little high schools, Joel would force-feed this repetitious menu of violence for so long that most people looked like they would never want to attend wrestling again upon leaving."

The brutality reached a pinnacle at Autumn Armageddon II, a show that *started* with a variation on a battle royal in which elimination came only when a wrestler bled. After three matches with local talent came a curiously misplaced technical masterpiece with Owen Hart against New Japan's Takayuki (now Takashi) Iizuka which was rumoured to have cost around $8,000 to put together and served no clear purpose other than to get Goodhart's name in the Japanese wrestling press. The card concluded with a dream trilogy of independent brawling: Terry Funk vs Kevin Sullivan, Gilbert and Madusa Miceli vs Cactus and Luna Vachon, and an Abdullah the Butcher vs The Sheik cage match.

While Goodhart's major shows continued to draw crowds of 1,500 or more, there was a fatal flaw in his business strategy: in his desire to put on the best show possible for his intended audience, he repeatedly spent so much on talent that even a sold-out show would lose money. The result was inevitable and Goodhart ceased activity in January of 1992, though not before racking up advance ticket sales for a show which would have featured everyone from Terry Gordy, Steve Williams, Doug Furnas and Dan Kroffat of All Japan to Shiro Koshinaka and Chris Benoit of New Japan, and even the 71-year-old former NWA and WWWF world champion Buddy Rogers.

But despite the ill-feeling among fans who found refunds difficult to come by, independent wrestling in Philadelphia was about to be kept alive by the most unlikely of sources.

2: The building at nowhere

"This isn't going to be the Tri-State Wrestling Alliance. You're not going to see people brawling all over the building during these cards." (Tod Gordon addressing the crowd at the first ECW show)

Tod Gordon's first involvement in professional wrestling had been expensive. The owner of a Philadelphia jewellery store, Carver W Reed, he had met Joel Goodhart after advertising on his radio show, and later became a silent partner in Tri-State. With the demise of the company, he wrote off his investment of $10,000 as a learning experience. But ring announcer Bob Artese had other ideas. He, along with wrestlers Larry Winters (who had booked Tri-State) and Stevie Wonderful persuaded Gordon to get a promoter's license and begin running monthly shows.

Picking the name Eastern Championship Wrestling, Gordon decided to limit his budget to one big star a show, but otherwise very little changed. The same crew of local wrestlers worked the shows, as did Tri-State referees John Finnegan and Jim Molineaux. The first ECW show, on 25 February 1992, took place at a regular Tri-State venue, the Original Sports Bar in Philadelphia. Stevie Richards worked the opener, a 20 minute draw with Jimmy Jannetty. The main event saw Johnny Hot Body and Larry Winters against DC Drake and JT Smith in a double disqualification. The only nationally known wrestler, Ivan Koloff, volunteered to put over anybody on the show, and his loss to Tony Stetson earned a four-page story in *Sports Review Wrestling*, one of the popular kayfabed newsstand magazines of the time. The only significant absence from the TWA crew was Mr Sandman, then a clean-cut babyface working under a surfer gimmick. In what should perhaps have been taken as a sign, his drunken behaviour after a previous show meant Sports Bar owner Mike Schmidt insisted he not appear on the debut show!

Despite Gordon's claims, building-wide brawls soon became a regular feature on the monthly ECW shows (which were drawing crowds in the 200-300 range), particularly after a shift of venue in

July to the Chestnut Cabaret rock club. Appealing to a more mature audience became a necessity after a disastrous first show at the building. It wasn't until he arrived on the day that Gordon discovered the venue's licensing barred anyone under 21. After giving refunds to all the minors who had bought tickets (and any accompanying adults), just 30 people remained for the show. When JT Smith refused to take a pay-off from the pitiful gate receipts, Gordon rewarded him with a full-time job at Carver W Reed.

There was never any serious thought given to expanding ECW at this point; Gordon himself said "Back then, my big idea was to one day run Delaware!" However, short of content, Sam Schroeder of Sports Channel Philadelphia (a friend of ECW assistant Matt Radico) approached Gordon in early 1993 with the idea of producing a TV show. Early shows were taped at a suburban community college, but from 14 May Gordon began running a South Philadelphia building officially known as Ritner Street Community Center, but better known as Viking Hall by its owners, the Philadelphia Viking Club. This was a local branch of the Mummers, a group that exists solely to organise the traditional 15,000-strong parade that takes place each New Year in the centre of Philadelphia. Wrestlers and fans alike would often struggle to find the building at the intersection of Swanson and Ritner Streets because the location did not officially exist: Viking members had simply paved over abandoned railroad tracks before building the venue.

The building, soon dubbed the ECW Arena, was a run-down facility used mainly for bingo (to fund the Viking Club), and was perfect for the rough-and-ready wrestling style; the owners gave free reign for Gordon and crew to cause as much mayhem as they wished as long as they repaired any damage. The first wrestling match held in the building was a handicap bout with Road Warrior Hawk defeating Don E Allen and The Samoan Warrior.

Gordon's original choice of booker for the TV show was Terry Funk, who not only turned down the offer, but warned Gordon to steer well clear of the wrestling business. He did agree to wrestle, and suggested the booking role go to Eddie Gilbert. Gilbert had been lobbying for a booking role even before the promotion had television, and his vast experience of weekly television in Memphis and booking spells in Alabama and for WCW made him a suitable candidate. The TV show in its early months had a traditional Southern style, with the main storyline being a 'merger' between Gilbert's 'Hot Stuff International' group (Gilbert, Don Muraco and Jimmy Snuka) and the 'Dangerous Alliance' stable of Paul E Dangerously, who had managed Gilbert in Alabama (and assisted in booking in his real-life persona of Paul Heyman).

One aspect of the show that stuck out, however, was the use of inside comments presumably aimed at the more dedicated Philadelphia fans (or simply put in for Gilbert and Heyman's own amusement). In the build-up to a Gilbert-Funk match, Dangerously claimed his lawyers would nullify the match contract announced by Gordon (who was the on-screen commissioner, the job title apparently chosen for a lame *Batman* joke). Dangerously asked Gordon "Don't you understand about my lawyers? What, are you from Oklahoma or something? Ask Ted and Jane about my lawyers?", referring to real-life clashes with former boss Bill Watts in Ted Turner's WCW. At an on-screen 'press conference' for another show, Gordon opened by addressing an 'off-screen' "Mr Meltzer and Mr Keller", a dig at the editors of the insider *Wrestling Observer* and *Pro Wrestling Torch* newsletters.

Once established on television, ECW held its first 'supershow', the 19 June Super Summer Sizzler '93, drawing around 500 to see Gilbert beat Funk in a bloody chain match to become the 'King of Philadelphia'. The finish involved referee Kevin Christian (the real-life son of Jerry Lawler) turn against Funk; after the match he claimed to be Freddie Gilbert, a "long-lost brother". The most notable incident of the show came in a 'Catfight Humiliation Match' between Terrible Tigra and Sandman's valet (and real-life wife) Peaches in which the loser would be the first woman stripped naked. Unfortunately neither woman agreed to Gordon's request to go so far, and the match ended when Tigra, stripped to her underwear, ran from the ring. As Peaches was declared the winner, the raucous male audience voiced their disapproval, only to roar in delight when another woman entered the ring and was promptly attacked by Tony Stetson and the Rockin' Rebel, exposing her unfeasibly large bosom. (The woman concerned, Angel Amaroso, later appeared in a bondage video titled *Angel Pays the Bills* which sold remarkable well among pubescent wrestling fans.) While parents of young children in attendance were understandably upset, the incident helped sales when the event became the first ECW video release.

The more cynical follower of the wrestling industry would probably have been wondering how long the notoriously hotheaded Gilbert would last in the role. During his career he earned a reputation for leaving promotions in bitter circumstances, most infamously the time he and brother Doug worked in Japan's W*ING group under masks as Freddie Krueger and Leatherface; fans were bemused when the rival monsters unmasked, flipped off the camera, condemned the promotion's management and lobbied for a job with All Japan Pro Wrestling!

In the summer of '93, Paul Heyman was officially working in a temporary role for ECW as he waited for Jim Crockett to begin attempts to run a third national promotion, the World Wrestling Network (Crockett was waiting out a five-year no-compete clause signed when he sold his company to Ted Turner in late 1988). While nothing had been formally agreed, the grapevine had it that Crockett's new group would work with ECW in some form. Gilbert's habitual paranoia left him convinced he was going to be double-crossed in some way, and it soon became simply a question of whether he would quit or get himself fired. Officially he resigned his role, but years later a story surfaced in the *Wrestling Observer* that he had made advances to Gordon's wife in an intentional act of career suicide; Gordon denies this is true.

Either way, ECW needed somebody new to take Gilbert's creative duties. And boy, did they ever get it.

3: Paul Heyman

"Does he make me crazy sometimes? Sure. When he's driving to the arena putting the matches together in the car on a little scrap of paper three inches by three inches." (Tod Gordon in the Pro Wrestling Torch*)*

You don't meet many 28 year old veterans in the wrestling business, but then you don't meet many people like Paul Heyman. He was in the business at the age of 13, rubbing shoulders (and barging elbows) with Bill Apter and George Napolitano as a ringside photographer. By 19 he was a television announcer for a Northeastern independent group. By 21 he was a manager, running for his life from a hostile Memphis crowd after Austin Idol defeated Jerry Lawler in a hair vs hair match. By 22 he'd booked two territories, Windy City and Continental. By 24 he was a manager on WCW's national TV. By 25 he'd been suspended.

Officially the split came over "philosophical differences" between Heyman and WCW boss Jim Herd. In reality, he took the heat after a plan to put the NWA title on Jerry Lawler to set up a title vs title match with WCW champion Lex Luger became public knowledge through an interview with non-WCW wrestler Eddie Gilbert. Lawler used this as a reason to pull out of the deal (though some believe he was simply escaping the inevitable loss to Luger at Starrcade) and Gilbert's friend Heyman was cited, accurately or not, as the source of the leak. A month later Heyman was back on TV with an infamous insider-oriented promo at Hallowe'en Havoc where he announced Rick Rude as the first member of his Dangerous Alliance, setting up a six month run heading the lead heel stable in the company.

Considering Heyman once threw a garbage can at Ric Flair during a heated debate, it was hardly surprising that things didn't work out between he and new WCW head Bill Watts; the record showed Heyman fired in early 1993 for attempted expense fraud but, whatever the truth, Heyman's rebellious streak was never have going to sat well with Watts' authoritarian stance.

That's not to say Heyman didn't have a way with people: he was always a skilled motivator. Countless wrestlers can tell stories of their frustration at his failure to return phone calls (ironic given his on-screen character's ever-present cellphone) leading to meetings where the angry man approaching Heyman would depart with a smile on their face, oblivious to the fact that the reason for their annoyance had not necessarily been addressed.

Such quick-thinking on Heyman's part also leant itself to a creative, if ramshackle, ability to put together wrestling storylines. As he was already producing interviews for the company, he was the obvious choice to take over Gilbert's booking duties. And his unconventional booking style soon helped establish some of the major acts that were to join then-champion Shane Douglas as the core of the company.

Ted Petty had just turned 40 years old. He was a 15 year-veteran who worked as a high-flying junior-heavyweight named the Cheetah Kid, and had already worked under Heyman's guidance on the first WWN house show as part of the masked Komodo Dragons team with Dean Malenko. Ted Petty was most definitely not an inner-city hip-hop gangster.

This didn't matter to Heyman. He teamed Petty (now 'Flyboy' Rocco Rock) with another independent wrestler, Johnny Rotten (now Johnny Grunge), in the opening match of the 18 September 1993 UltraClash event. A memorable squash of Jason Knight and Ian Rotten established the new team of Public Enemy and set in motion perhaps the ultimate case of Heyman making the most of his talent; indeed, Heyman himself has said Public Enemy were the only act for which he took full creative credit. Through cutting-edge interviews (supposedly filmed in 'the hood' but actually in the streets surrounding the ECW Arena) laced with pop-culture references and insider humour, and a hard-edged blood-laden ring style, the pair somehow convinced many that they were the best team in the country. Later spells in WCW and the WWF suggested this might have been a case of the sizzle outshining the steak.

But the debut of Public Enemy was far from the only notable event at UltraClash. The scheduled feature match of Eddie Gilbert and Abdullah the Butcher against Terry Funk and Stan Hansen had been revised with Kevin Sullivan taking Gilbert's place. Which made it even stranger when Gilbert arrived at the arena and asked if he could set up a merchandise stand and run-in at the end of the match to attack Funk, promoting a planned feud between the pair in Texas. While Heyman agreed to this, he didn't authorise Gilbert to then grab the microphone, turn himself babyface, say farewell to the fans, and attempt to sell his ring gear. Ironically the idea of a wrestler going beyond his arranged activities would, in entirely fictional form, become a recurring theme in ECW booking over the years.

The tag match itself was predictably violent (the notoriously short-sighted Hansen even 'choked' Gordon, mistaking him for the ring announcer), but was topped by the final bout in which the Headhunters took on Miguel Perez Jr and Crash The Terminator (who later became a Boricua and Hugh Morrus respectively) with a baseball bat a legal weapon. The crowning point of the contest came when one of the Headhunters was thrown through the plasterboard wall that divided the main arena from the dressing room. Fans looking through the new hole were greeted by the unforgettable sight of Abdullah the Butcher sitting in nothing but his underpants, smoking a cigar.

This wasn't the only incident of its type. Advertising salesman and former *Pro Wrestling Illustrated* staffer Joey Styles had been brought in earlier for an announcing tryout by Heyman and was similarly lacking in outer garments upon his first meeting with Gordon. Unfortunately Gordon knew nothing of his appointment and understandably was bemused to see this near-naked, glasses-wearing non-wrestler backstage.

Fortunately for Styles his tryout was successful and he was hired to replace former announcer Jay Sulli by the time of ECW's Bloodfeasts tapings. On 1 and 2 October, the promotion taped six TV shows, now under the banner of NWA Eastern Championship Wrestling, Gordon having joined the National Wrestling Alliance at its annual meeting in September.

The first night was main-evented by Terry Funk defeating Jimmy Snuka for the TV title in a cage match, but it was an undercard bout which stole the show. Sabu, the nephew of the Sheik, was already a regular in Japan's FMW group but, despite pushing 30, had only recently gained a US reputation after matches with the

Lightning Kid (Sean 'X-Pac' Waltman) and Jerry Lynn in Minnesota. Heyman responded by putting him in a match with fellow ECW debutant Tasmaniac, a skilled amateur wrestler now performing as a near-Neanderthal character. Sabu was hastily repackaged with a Hannibal Lector mask and brought to the ring on a gurney by a handler (who would later be known as 911) and managed by Heyman in his Dangerously role. The bout saw the pair brawl across the building, and Sabu celebrated his win by moonsaulting through a table; unlike those who later imitated him, he chose to do so without the formality of placing an opponent in his way. The next time the pair wrestled on TV would be more than three years later, on a far greater stage.

On the second night of the tapings, Taz defeated another new ECW wrestler, Tommy Dreamer, who at the time was a muscular smiling youngster wearing suspenders; the very definition of a white meat babyface. On the same show Sabu, in what would appear to be relatively spontaneous booking, took the ECW title from Shane Douglas in an impromptu match.

The shows taped at Bloodfeasts were a full-fledged example of Heyman's new style of television. Instead of the one-take live or 'as live' events of the territories, or the slick syndicated shows of the WWF and WCW with their rigid template formats, ECW TV was an MTV-style fast-paced hour with heavy use of music videos and packages. The long-haired high-energy 'Matty In The House' (Matt Radico) presented frantic pitches for upcoming events. One week the show finished and cut to the SportsChannel logo only for Jason Knight, the self-proclaimed 'Sexiest Man Alive', to burst through and ask viewers how they liked his new suit, a spot conceived by Gordon's eight-year-old daughter! Another episode opened with clips 'from a local TV news show' of Public Enemy being arrested. A police officer explained they were arrested under their wrestling names because they failed to provide identification, and said their recent actions were assault beyond the acceptable realms of pro wrestling. As he was led off, Johnny Grunge asked for "a cell next to Vince", referring to the recent indictment of WWF chief McMahon on steroid distribution charges.

Back in the ring, Sabu scored the pin at the first November

to Remember show as he teamed with Road Warrior Hawk to beat Funk and mystery partner King Kong Bundy; the win gave Sabu the TV title, making him a double-champion. A month later, at Holiday Hell, Funk took Sabu's heavyweight title in a no-disqualification match, though at this point in ECW's development, the stipulation was frankly superfluous. The show was best remembered for an ill-fated 'body count' match between Rocco Rock and Pat Tanaka. Partners Grunge and Paul Diamond were locked in a cage which was primed to explode at the 15 minute mark, an incentive for both competitors to win the match and secure their man's freedom. Unfortunately a security guard unaware of the set-up had mistakenly knocked over the container of gunpowder and the resulting explosion resembled a bad case of flatulence in both execution and reaction.

Gordon apologised to the fans, admitting that "we screwed up" and vowed the promotion would always live up to its promises in the future. Such refreshing frankness wasn't always the case though. Gordon claimed the show had drawn just over a thousand fans, while adding that a show earlier in the month set up an attendance record of 1,492, figures fans seized upon as evidence ECW was the future; WCW at this time was drawing as little as 600 in its hometown Atlanta. However, footage of the ECW Arena set-up at the time shows three rows of seats and three rows of bleachers, around 20 seats across on each side of the ring. Even allowing for the bleachers being more densely packed than the equivalent seating, it is clear the crowds at the time could barely have broken the 500 mark.

Still, exaggeration is considered a healthy form of business in the 'perception is reality' world of pro wrestling, and ECW's image as a significant force was about to take another step forwards.

4: The Night The Line Was Crossed

"Before the match, I saw Heyman kneeling on the floor, praying. He said the match would either make or break the company." (ECW assistant and future Ring Of Honor booker Gabe Sapolsky)

For every cultural movement, there is a defining moment. For ECW, it was 5 February 1994 at the ECW Arena.

The show started with Mr Hughes squashing local cult hero (and early 80s WWF regular) Sal Bellomo, followed by Sandman and Tommy Cairo beating the Rockin' Rebel and the then-solo Pitbull in a double dog-collar match; after the bout, Sandman mistakenly shoved down valet Peaches, which was to play an important part in a future angle. The Bruise Brothers fought Public Enemy in an arena-wild brawl (with Rocco Rock literally bounced off a wall), and Jimmy Snuka pinned Tommy Dreamer, but not before Dreamer kicked out of the Superfly squash in a booking attempt to establish his character's toughness (the sign "Wet Dreamer" summing up the crowd's view of him at the time). Pat Tanaka and the Sheik overcame Tasmaniac and Sullivan in a match ending with Sheik throwing a fireball, and he and Sullivan doing their utmost to destroy a vending machine. And Mike Awesome stunned the crowd by destroying JT Smith in a second under two minutes, highlighted by a dive that crushed Smith into the guardrail and most closely resembled a guided missile. The display was so, well, awesome that to this day most viewers forget that Smith actually won the bout with a small package; an enraged Awesome responded by powerbombing the referee twice, climbing to and breaking the top rope, and hurling the remnants of the turnbuckle onto the downed official.

And that was just the undercard.

The main event of The Night The Line Was Crossed was not the first ever three-way match. A round-robin series between three wrestlers had taken place as far back as the late 19th century, bringing together experts in the styles of catch-as-catch can, collar-and-elbow, and side-hold (a British style involving wearing a harness for gripping). Smoky Mountain Wrestling held a three-way nine-man match at April 1993's Bluegrass Brawl with all men legal at once, while four-corner team matches (requiring tags) were common in 1980s Mid South. But while Mexico had its 'triangular' matches, and Canada's Stampede group had 'Bermuda Triangle' bouts, this was the first high-profile United States match where three men competed at the same time under traditional pinfall rules. (A 1977 bout with Fritz Von Erich, Bruiser Brody and the Sheik had elimination only by bodyslam, in or out of the ring.)

The match, pitting ECW champion Funk against Shane Douglas and Sabu, was also the first 60 minute draw to gain national attention since Nick Bockwinkle's AWA title match with Curt Hennig shown on ESPN on New Year's Eve 1986. Heyman's aim was to establish Douglas as a legitimate classic-style champion, while adding Funk's legendary status and Sabu's embodiment of a futuristic-style into the mix.

He didn't need to worry. The elimination bout started with Sabu and Douglas alone for the first 15 minutes (had either man won, they would have faced Funk immediately), with Douglas' valet Sherri Martel, and Sabu's manager Dangerously both floored before the opening bell. Thirteen minutes in, Douglas evaded a Sabu Asai-moonsault, leaving Sabu to crash onto a table and, once Funk had entered, be carried to the back. He didn't return until past the half-hour mark, with an important part of the bout's legacy being that Douglas was the only man to wrestle the full hour. As well as then-innovative spots involving all three-men (most notably a Funk sleeper on Douglas, who in turn had a sleeper on Sabu), the match was kept lively with liberal interference by Martel, Dangerously, 911 and Axl & Ian Rotten, who teamed as the Bad Breed.

Future *Wrestling Lariat* editor Dave Scherer later told of an incident where a woman, stood on a chair to get a better view, slipped to the ground. Her boyfriend is alleged to have responded by pointing out that the call of two minutes to time limit had just been made and that he would therefore wait before going to her assistance!

What few remember is that when the final bell rang, the crowd let out a hearty boo at the absence of a winner. But only a few seconds later, they broke into a legitimate standing ovation at the efforts all three had made.

Just as important as the match to the event's legacy was the post-match interview, filmed as if it were a press conference at a nearby hotel. It began with Terry Funk 'addressing the media':

"You know, I want to tell you people something. I love wrestling. I've loved it all my life and I'm gonna tell you that I'm not real proud of the way that it's evolved in a lotta places in the country. I don't believe that the WCW is worth a damn. I think it ridicules my profession and I think that we have a bunch of people that don't have any respect for the profession running those organisations and the WWF. I'm not talking about the guys individually, but I'm talking about the way that they have belittled my profession because I think that I'm an athlete and I think that I was out there tonight with a hell of a pair of competitors in that ring that were not.... not only wrestling, they were wrestling with their heart.
"I don't particularly like the opponents that I was against tonight, but they damn sure gave the fans their money's worth, and I think that I did too. I think that ECW has come a long way. I think that you got guys that have come from ... from nowhere... I'm talking about the Sandman; I'm talking about the other guys; I'm talking about the old timers; I'm talking about Jimmy Snuka; We've all seen this organisation grow and I'm really proud of it. And I am very proud to be wearing this belt around my waist. I told you people before 'Hey: I am an old man' but I am making my stand. And I'm making it here in ECW and those other people can go to hell. Because we're here and we're here to stay. And we're going to become an organisation that's not producing something for kids. We're athletic and I think we are a sport and I know that we've got a lot of guys here that are wrestling their heart out. I'm not trying to take anything away from anybody else, but I have respect for Shane Douglas, and I have respect for Sabu, and I have respect for all the guys that are here with ECW and I wanna thank all you people out there for being hardcore fans and that's what we're playing to, the hardcore fans. I want you to know that I love you and thank you very much for supporting me. I really appreciate it."

[Douglas walks in, accompanied by Sherri Martel. Its worth

remembering that at this point Douglas was still best known for having being part of the clean-cut, happy-go-lucky pretty-boy babyface team the Dynamic Dudes, who were memorably savaged by the Philadelphia crowd at the NWA Hallowe'en Havoc '89 pay-per-view.]

"Mr Gordon. I gotta couple words for you. Tonight I took the Living Legend, so called self-proclaimed, Terry Funk and I beat his ass right in the centre of the ring. I took Sabu, the crazy man of wrestling and I beat his ass right in the centre of the ring. I sent 'em both back to the dressing room, Mr Gordon, and as a result of that, I want you to declare me right now, in front of this TV camera and in front of the whole world as the ECW Heavyweight champion to prove that I am the Franchise. Sherri saw it. The whole world saw it. Philadelphia, you witnessed it live. Professional wrestling as it should be: ass-kicking, take no names, beat the hell outta whoever's in front of you. Terry Funk, I smashed your knee to oblivion. When I took you with that chair outside the ring, even the crazy man Sabu and his people looked at me and said 'Oh my God, it's the end of an era. Finally put to rest the fucking Funk family"

[Tod Gordon yells at Shane for his language.]

"I don't give a shit. You keep your mouth shut. You keep your mouth shut. You can fire me if you want to. You can take me out of this territory if you want to, but you can't stop the Franchise. Someplace, sometime I will be heavyweight champion. Now as it goes for you Mr. Styles and anybody else and all you other sons of bitches sitting out here today. I've had it up to here. I've come to Philadelphia and seen pieces of shit in the audience hold up signs and call me every name in the book. I've seen people outside the arena call me names and say things about my family and say things about Sherri. I've seen people..."

[Terry Funk walks onto the scene with the belt.]

"And what do you want? And what do you want?"

Funk: *What's wrong with you? Are you some kind of a fool*

or what?

Douglas: *Am I some kind of a fool? What are you, out here? All I've got to ask you Mr. Funk: what you were 10 years ago was a legend. What you are today is an old man. A shell of yourself. Look at the legs. [Laughs.] After tonight certainly they aren't what they used to be. Muhammed Ali knows what it's like when the legs go. Look at your face. Take a look in the mirror around you. Ask the media. How's his face look? You've been beat to a pulp. Now I've been beat up tonight. Take a look Philadelphia. Look at his face. Look at my face. Look who's standing tall. Terry Funk, you were a beaten man tonight.*

Funk: *I've listened to you call me an old man. I've listened to you ridicule me and yeah, maybe I've had better days. But I don't think you have any right to come in here and say that. I came out here and I paid compliments to you. I paid compliments to Sabu. I paid compliments to everybody because I think that you're a good athlete and a heckuva guy. But you didn't walk outta there with this thing around your waist and you know you didn't.*

Douglas: *Terry Funk you listen to this...*

Funk*: Don't call me an old man.*

Douglas: *I gave you your time, now you let me talk. As the franchise of ECW I have every right to come out here and say what I want to say. Paying compliments to Shane Douglas and paying compliments to Sabu doesn't pay the bills. The gold pays the bills. Now I want Tod Gordon right here and now to declare me the champion because you were carried out of the arena tonight by your own men and that's not a champion to me. Sabu was carried out of the arena by his own men. Both at the hands of the Franchise. To me that means that I am the heavyweight champion. No Ifs, Ands or Buts about it, Mr Funk.*

Funk: *You want this belt so bad? I've said earlier that I've drawn the line. I tell you something. You've made a big mistake...*

Douglas: *Don't put your finger in my face.*

Funk: *I won't put my finger in your face. I have no intention of doing that. But your biggest mistake was calling me an old man because first of all, what is it gonna look like whenever this old man* [smirks] *whips your butt? And as far as this belt is concerned... you can have this belt. I'm giving it to you.*

Douglas: *You're giving it to me?*

Funk: *I'm giving it to you. Go on, take it.* [Hands him the belt.] *Isn't that silly? That is so silly. No, no Tod. Be quiet. I'm sorry because I know that's not very respectful to you. But I'm telling you, you take this belt. And you know why you can take that belt? Because it's gonna be the biggest thrill for me on the [next show] to take it back from you. That's what's gonna give me the biggest elation. Because I'm gonna show you that this old man is not as easy to push around as you think he is, and you should found that out tonight.*

Douglas: *Terry Funk...*

Funk: *I know, don't put my finger in your chest. I won't even touch your chest.*

Douglas: *Terry Funk, you don't have to give me this belt. You don't have to give me the belt you old piece of shit! You don't have to give me the fucking belt. Because I'm gonna take it from you.* [Throws belt at Funk and hits him in the head.] *How about that? How about that you son of a bitch? Huh?*

[Funk slaps him in the head and a brawl ensues. Cameras fade to black]

The newsletter buzz about the show helped spread the word about ECW, but it was the home video release that was the breakthrough point for the company. The first full event released other than Summer Sizzler (though several compilations were available), it pioneered a series of tapes that sold enough copies to help keep Gordon afloat. And the legal sales were dwarfed by the tape's success on the bootleg market: as far afield as Britain it was the first imported tape to sell in the hundreds, and its influence was strong that readers of newsstand magazine *PowerSlam* voted it show of the year despite it not being legally available in the country.

5: The fans

"The audience was the story. The audience interaction was ECW." (Paul Heyman, The Rise and Fall of ECW *DVD)*

As tape buyers began watching the Arena show tapes, they would notice there was something different about this venue. Not only did they come to know the wrestlers, but they soon recognised many of the fans who would sit in the same seats every time, thanks in part to Club ECW, a 'season ticket' package where you could reserve a regular seat by paying for four shows at a time. The most iconic spectator was John Bailey, better known as Hat Guy for his ever-present straw hat. He helped take tickets at the door in return for his prime location dead centre of the front row looking towards the hard camera. He became such a part of arena tradition that his taking of his seat and placing his hat on his head became the unofficial signal that the opening bell was imminent. Viewers even followed him to other promotions with notable appearances at WCW Slamboree '94 (where Terry Funk stole and elbowed his hat) and WWF King Of The Ring '95 (where he showed his displeasure at seeing Savio Vega wrestle four times in one night, with King Mabel pulling double-duty).

The spot to Bailey's immediate left (from the camera's view) was the permanent home of Paul 'Sign Guy' Mellows, whose handwritten signs with caustic insider comments often voiced the viewer's own opinion. Mellows often had such a prophetic ability to hold up signs fitting in with angles as they happened that the cynic might well speculate he was privy to insider information. But it worked both ways: during the first meeting of Cactus Jack and Sabu, his sign proclaimed 'This is Hardcore Heaven'; the following Arena show bore the very same title. His suggestion to 'Cane Dewey', referring to Mick Foley's young son, became a key part of Foley's legendary 'anti-hardcore' promos. And Mellows quite literally became part of the show when the Dudley Clan gained a new member, Sign Guy Dudley. The pair even feuded by the medium of signs until the rivalry got so out of control that it appeared the basic concepts of pro wrestling's operation had been forgotten by some. (According to Raven, Sign Guy Dudley was created after Mellows made the mistake of using insider terminology when he saw Stevie Richards in a public gym and it was felt he should be put in his place.)

Mellows was also responsible for a sign reading "I pledge allegiance to the wrestlers of ECW and to the violence for which we demand, one promotion, under Tod, politically incorrect, with broken tables and barbed wire for all", which was later turned into a T-shirt.

The third of the most recognisable characters was a man named Lenny who, thanks to his sunglasses and long black hair and beard was popularly known as 'Beard Dude' or 'Faith No More Guy'. He was also a regular at televised shows from other promotions, most notably when he travelled to California for WrestleMania XII and gave his verdict on the scoreless Iron Man match with Shawn Michaels and Bret Hart by extending his middle finger to mark the closing bell.

Other fans became recognisable to long-time viewers. 'Hat Guy' was usually accompanied by another man in a Hawaiian shirt with grey hair and a moustache who resembled the ageing AWA star The Crusher. Once the Dudley characters took off, a couple of dedicated fans who sat a few rows behind 'Hat Guy' and company would always dress in their likeness, even long after Buh Buh's heel turn, at which point a Dudley fan was probably in more danger than the wrestlers themselves from overly-passionate fans. A red-headed man with a Jimmy Valiant beard could usually be found to the left of the hard camera's picture. Sat in the bleachers was a colourful bare-chested character nicknamed 'Dreads' whose surplus of testosterone made it all the more notable when he broke down in tears after Eddie Guerrero and Dean Malenko's final match in the arena. Sitting to the right of the ring behind the timekeeper's table, clad in glasses and a baseball cap, was Tom Misnik who, as the self-proclaimed 'Mr ECW', became the company's head cheerleader online, particularly in the rec.sport.pro-wrestling newsgroup, and later organised two internet fan conventions each year. (With a target audience of males in their teens and twenties, the internet was a particularly effective marketing and feedback tool for a group aiming to build an 'underground movement' audience.) On the corner of the front row and the aisleway was a woman with strawberry-blonde hair who demonstrated her support for Shane Douglas long after it was advisable to do so in a hostile building. And perhaps the most extreme fan was the one who had the ECW initials tattooed on his arm, making his later apparent falling out with the company all the more unfortunate.

So much of what is now familiar at independent wrestling events was pioneered by the fans at the ECW Arena. Spontaneous chants would be picked up by the majority of the audience, not simply the name of the babyface, but commentary on the individuals in the ring, the product, or the industry itself. What started as a storyline reaction to JT Smith intentionally missing moves became a controversial regular activity: any wrestler making a mistake would be greeted with chants of "You fucked up!" even when the error had led to serious injury. And the audience was far from consistent: it was not unusual for a departing wrestler to be greeted with a chorus of "You sold out!" on their way to the ring and "Please don't go!" as they left.

But while the Philadelphia fans voiced their appreciation for attitude, effort and talent (arguably in that order), fans elsewhere were more likely to fall into the clichéd response of being little more than bloodthirsty. In particular, New York fans gained a reputation for an unhealthy preference for brutality, even booing a Rey Misterio Jr vs Juventud Guerrera match (which, in its rematch form the following night in Philadelphia, was arguably among the best in company history). Perhaps the most astounding case came in June 1996 when fans bombarded performers at a WCW event in Manhattan with ECW chants; as Konnan pointed out, they could have gone to an ECW event in Middletown, less than 70 miles away, which was taking place at the same time. This is not to say, however, that New York fans weren't an asset to the company; indeed, the atmosphere in the Elks Lodge, Queens was so raucous and television-friendly that the company continued taping shows there long after it was clear even a sell-out in the venue would not be profitable.

Chants and signs weren't the only form of audience interaction. While the line was drawn at physically attacking wrestlers, face-to-face confrontations were not unusual (particularly at the peak of the Dudleys heel run), while providing weapons for wrestlers to use became part of the ECW experience, which was tremendous news for a miscellaneous goods store just down the road from the ECW Arena. What started as a moment of quirkiness when a fan handed Cactus Jack a frying pan turned into a phenomenon that saw fans walking into the building with everything from cheese graters to computer keyboards and from video tapes to video recorders. Eventually it got so out of hand that weapons would be confiscated at the door and placed into a garbage can for New Jack to use during his matches.

While most fans knew better then to pass the guardrail, there were a couple of occasions when getting into the ring was encouraged. At the end of the Hardcore Heaven '95 event, Public Enemy invited fans into the ring to dance along to their music, providing a memorable closing scene on the home video. A week later they attempted to recreate the scene in Tampa only for the weight of the fans to cause the ring to collapse! Fortunately nobody was injured by the incident.

But perhaps the legacy of the ECW fans was the chant of the promotion's initials (or as it eventually became in abbreviated form, "E-C-Dub") which passed from being the traditional close to a show to becoming the universal approval for any stiff blow or jaw-dropping dive, even if it took place in another promotion. Konnan's AAA shows in Tijuana were the first where wrestlers tried to prompt the crowd into a less-than-spontaneous chant of the promotion's own initials, and years later it is one of many ploys used by independent groups (most notably "cee-zee-dubya") to emulate the fan response and passion of the ECW Arena faithful. Indeed, formulaic chants are now little more than a cliché for fans who truly believe they are part of the show.

In the ECW, they were.

6: Character assimilation

"There were people in that converted bingo hall who literally thought they were going to see someone die." (Mick Foley on his match with Sabu, Have A Nice Day)

An ECW without Paul Heyman or Joey Styles today seems inconceivable. But in the spring of 1994, it could easily have come to pass.

Styles departed in May when his day job made it impractical to drive to Philadelphia each week and add his commentary to the TV show throughout the night, returning straight to work the following morning. He was at first replaced with Jay Sulli, and then Willie 'Scoop' Watts, a black gentleman whose screen name was a less-than-subtle dig at a certain former WCW boss with controversial views on racial discrimination. His commentary work was generally judged to be even lamer than the gag and, in a compromise to ensure Styles' return, production of the show was moved to the New York home of producer Ron Buffone (who doubled as a cameraman). While Styles' travel problems were eased, through-the-night production was still the usual practice.

The television shows at the time were usually taped at the ECW Arena on the Sunday afternoon following each main Saturday show. While the company ran occasional spot shows, including one in Valley Forge where Shane Douglas took the ECW title from Terry Funk in a War Games-style match, the majority of major bouts took place on the Arena shows. Most fans outside of Philadelphia did not start trading television shows until later in the year when the company expanded its TV network, so the home video releases were the main way to keep up with the promotion.

Meanwhile Heyman was heavily involved in Jim Crockett's World Wrestling Network group, which taped its first show at the Manhattan Center on 28 February, highlighted by a Sabu-Funk match. Rumour at the time had Heyman departing ECW after its next Arena show, with Kevin Sullivan pencilled in as the replacement booker. Fortunately for history, Crockett dropped his idea of national television (which would have included taping high-definition TV almost a decade before the technology caught on), relocating to the South before fizzling out. Not only did ECW retain the services of Heyman, but they benefited from several of his ideas which he would most likely have saved for the national stage.

One such concept was the 'Wrestling School Dropout', the supreme underdog. Among the ring crew of the time were three inexperienced trainees of Sonny Blaze named Mike Norman, Paul Lauria and John Watson. All three eventually worked for the company, but it was the latter who received the gimmick. While there was some talk of naming the character 'The Ultimate Worrier', Heyman instead took the surname of Maryland promoter Dennis Whippreicht (whose MEWF group had co-promoted with ECW the previous November), and Watson's own middle name, to produce Mikey Whipwreck. After a series of one-sided defeats, Whipwreck (who came to the ring to Beck's *Loser*, clad in an oversized *Dungeons & Dragons* shirt) scored a fluke victory to take the TV title from The Pitbull. Having assumed everyone telling him the finish was playing a practical joke, Whipwreck's look of astonishment at winning the belt was particularly convincing! Mikey would then begin a run of upset wins over 911, Rockin' Rebel, both Pitbulls, Sandman, and Chad Austin, with every win coming by disqualification when his opponent went too far in the beating.

911 himself was a character taken to the other extreme. He became known not for his (less than stellar) matches, but for his surprise appearances. After a fast count against him by referee John 'Pee Wee' Moore, he returned on the next show to chokeslam Moore and, for good measure, both Austin and Don E Allen who were about to start their match. 911 was soon built up as the indestructible chokeslam machine who could appear at any moment. The 'smart fans' of Philadelphia were willing to forget the obvious question of how his 'spontaneous run-ins' were eventually always accompanied by his ring music (*Frankenstein* by The Edgar Winter Band) as the theme's opening notes usually prompted one of the biggest cheers of the night. And this was several years before Steve Austin's shattering glass or the Undertaker's tombing bell provided a similar function in the WWF.

As it happened, perhaps the mc
ECW was still several months from be
Metallica's *Enter Sandman*, the wrestl
using Elton John's *The Bitch Is Back* i
the inarguably named Woman. But
development. All concerned had
character as Jim Fullington portrayed
returned to the locker room to revert to his na...
loudmouthed self, and even the fans picked up on it. ...
told the *Pro Wrestling Torch*, "We did one angle where Sandma...
in and saved a jobber who was getting killed by [Pitbull 1]. He made
the save and the entire audience started yelling 'Sandman sucks!'
They wanted to see this guy keep beating the jobber up."

Now officially a heel, Sandman began smoking on his way
to the ring (a move which took Gordon several months to persuade
Heyman to approve), while intimating that he was a pimp and that
former customer Tommy Cairo had outstanding bills to pay. But it
was an event on the other side of the world that made the character.
American youth Michael Fay was arrested in Singapore for
vandalising a car and, after two months of diplomatic rows, received
his sentence of six blows with a Singapore cane on 5 May. Just nine
days later, Sandman and Woman took on Cairo and Sandman's
former valet Peaches in a topical match where the loser would suffer
the same fate. Having been humiliatingly pinned by Peaches,
Sandman took three strokes before Woman threw powder in her eyes
and Sandman grabbed the cane and destroyed Cairo. Predictably the
fans loved it.

A month later the two men met in a rematch where the cane
was placed atop a pole for either man to grab. Having long abandoned
the rules of fair play, Sandman used a second cane, earning himself a
disqualification, which seemed of little consequence as he continued
his assault, pausing only to relight his cigarette. And at the following
show, Sandman took the victory in a match where both men were
legally armed with a cane, giving him victory in the feud and
prompting him to carry the cane at all times. All that remained was to
add a can of beer to the cigarette and the character was complete. It's
worth remembering that a day after the Cairo feud finished, Hulk
Hogan won the WCW title, while Bret Hart was reigning WWF

, Sandman's character, while officially a heel, was greeted ECW fans as the embodiment of just how different the audience and product was in 'their' promotion.

On the other hand, Sabu (now freed from the gurney gimmick) had developed just as strong a case as the figurehead of ECW. His growing reputation for apparent insanity received a boost when he cut open a hand while on tour in Japan and, rather than get it stitched up, sealed it shut with Krazy Glue (an American form of Super Glue), having vaguely remembered a similar trick from TV's *MacGyver*. It turned out that it wasn't just furniture destruction and somersault variations where Sabu was ahead of his time; four years later the Closure Medical Corporation announced the development of DermaBond, a glue-like method for healing cuts.

Back in Philadelphia, Sabu's opponents were not limited to the ECW roster. He teamed with Bobby Eaton to beat Funk and Arn Anderson (the two WCW wrestlers were believed to have been allowed to take the booking in return for WCW getting advertising slots on the ECW TV show). And at the following show he took on Cactus Jack in what was truly an independent dream match, ending with Sabu taking the win after Dangerously cracked his opponent in the head with a cellphone. Cactus responded by cutting a controversial interview, spitting on his WCW tag title belt and throwing it to the ground, in a piece of promotional activity hardly appreciated by his Atlanta bosses. And they probably weren't overly impressed when he returned to the Arena and took on Terry Funk in a match that went to a brief no-contest when Public Enemy interfered, causing fans to bombard the ring with around 150 chairs in a scene that became an iconic moment in the TV show's opening (and caused terrified referee John Finnegan to take refuge under the ring!)

That's not to say anyone should have been surprised by the response, as it directly followed on from the previous month's show. Having successfully concluded their rivalry with the Bruise Brothers, Public Enemy's build had continued with a win over Terry and Dory Funk Jr, which prompted a no-rope barbed-wire rematch. On what was perhaps over-enthusiastically reported as a 130 degree evening, the aptly named Heatwave show ended with Terry Funk having a flattened garbage can strapped to his chest with reels of barbed wire and acting as a human battering ram. Though he fell in defeat, he had the final say by encouraging fans to throw their chairs into the ring; within moments the bloodied Rock and Grunge could barely be seen beneath the mountain of furniture and barbed wire.

As the crowd of mainly males in their twenties and thirties saluted the climax with a standing ovation and the traditional chant of "ECW! ECW!", officials began a frantic effort to clear up the debris.

Stood outside the building were a line of elderly ladies waiting for the midnight bingo game.

7: The Double-Cross

"It was the right thing to do for business. Whether it was the right thing to do karmically, I'm not so sure." (Raven, Forever Hardcore*)*

The NWA was already as good as dead.

What had once been an alliance of promoters that controlled the entire industry in the United States was now down to six members. Of those, just three (Tod Gordon, Jim Crockett and New Jersey's Dennis Coraluzzo) were promoting in the US, with Australia's Larry O'Day, New Zealand's Steve Rickard and lawyer Bob Trobich making up the numbers. With WCW having resigned from the alliance in September 1993, the NWA was left with no champion and limited exposure.

The public events of what followed were simple. The reality was far more complicated.

With its growing TV exposure, ECW was the logical host for a tournament to crown a new NWA champion on 27 August 1994. The event featured four ECW wrestlers (Shane Douglas, Tazmaniac, Too Cold Scorpio and 911) and four outsiders (Dean Malenko, Osamu Nishimura, Doink and Chris Benoit). The final came down to Douglas defeating Scorpio in a clean, traditional NWA title-style match. Following the win, Douglas said:

"In the tradition of the Lou Theszs, the Jack Briscos, the Dory Funk Jrs, the Terry Funks, the Harley Races, the Barry Windhams, the.... Ric Flairs. I accept this heavyweight title... Wait a second. Wait a second... Of the Kerry Von Erich. Of the fatman himself, Dusty Rhodes... [looks upwards] *This is it tonight, Dad...* [looks at the belt] *God, that's beautiful... and Rick Steamboat... and they can all... KISS... MY... ASS!* [Throws belt to the ground] *Because I am not the man who accepts the torch to be handed down to me from an organisation that died, RIP, seven years ago. The Franchise, Shane Douglas, is the man who ignites the new flame of the sport of professional wrestling.* [Picks up ECW title belt] *Tonight, before*

God and my father as witness, I declare myself, the Franchise, as the new ECW heavyweight champion of the world! We have set out to change the face of professional wrestling, so tonight let the new era begin. The era of the sport of professional wrestling. The era of the Franchise. The era of the ECW!" [Crowd begins ECW chant.]

Three days later, ECW's TV show aired, featuring clips of the tournament, the final in full, and Douglas' speech. The scene then cut to the dressing room where Coraluzzo said:

"I'm on my way to a conference call with NWA members Jim Crockett and Steve Rickard. What happened tonight was a disgrace. I'm disappointed. Shane Douglas is the NWA Champion. He threw the belt down. He had no right to do that. And remember one thing: ECW is an NWA member and they are under our jurisdiction. I'm going to the conference call right now and all I can say is Shane Douglas is the world's champion, the NWA champion whether he likes it or not. And we have another problem to be taken care of: he also has the ECW championship and the possibility remains of him being stripped of both of them."

Following this, the camera cut to Gordon in his office:

"A representative of the NWA board of directors took it upon himself to inform me that they have the power to force NWA Eastern Championship Wrestling not to recognise 'The Franchise' Shane Douglas as the World's Heavyweight Champion. Well, as of noon today, I have folded NWA Eastern Championship Wrestling. In its place will be ECW: Extreme Championship Wrestling and we recognise 'The Franchise' Shane Douglas as our World's Heavyweight Champion. We encourage any wrestler in the world today to come to the ECW to challenge for that belt. This is the ECW: Extreme Championship Wrestling, changing the face of wrestling."

The show finished with Public Enemy standing by an ECW banner, spraying out the word Eastern and replacing it with EXTREME, adding that "if you thought we were hardcore before, now we're going to take it to the extreme."

A week later, Coraluzzo issued a statement saying the NWA had "declared the recent heavyweight championship tournament held by ECW null and void. This is due to the conduct of Tod Gordon and the unprofessional attitude of Shane Douglas. Shane Douglas will never be recognised as a former NWA champion."

The story seemed simple enough: Heyman and Gordon had double-crossed Coraluzzo and the NWA to further establish ECW's rebel image.

But there was more to the story than met the eye.

* Gordon and Coraluzzo had co-promoted a show in January 1993 as part of a convention organised by the Legends of Wrestling group. This was the event where Eddie Gilbert first raised the possibility of coming in to book for ECW.

* The pair had an unofficial agreement that Gordon would not promote in New Jersey and Coraluzzo would not promote in Pennsylvania.

* According to Coraluzzo, Gordon then hired Kevin Lawler to promote ECW events outside Philadelphia and advised him that he was free to run shows in New Jersey. ECW did not run in New Jersey during Lawler's time in the role.

* On 31 October 1993, Legends of Wrestling president Mark Stern was the public face of a show in Bensalem, Pennsylvania (20 minutes from Philadelphia). However, it was little secret that Coraluzzo was involved in the show, which was run with his Pennsylvania promoter's licence.

* Coraluzzo ran a Sabu vs Chris Benoit match in Cherry Hills, New Jersey (across the river from Philadelphia) on 26 February 1994. Gordon said this was a breach of their agreement as they had said they would not use each other's talent on rival shows. Coraluzzo said this did not apply, because Sabu was a free agent. (Sabu had appeared in a feature match at the Bensalem show.)

* ECW debuted in New Jersey on 17 June 1994.

* The pair later blamed each other for their falling-out. Gordon claimed Coraluzzo attempted to get ECW shows cancelled before the tournament. Coraluzzo later admitted (indeed, boasted) of having done so, but dated these actions to 1995 and 1996. He claimed Gordon started the rivalry by acting "like the Emperor of Pennsylvania." He added that "Gordon's a super-flyweight and I'm a super-heavyweight when it comes to fucking with people." Gordon said he had caught Coraluzzo and a colleague letting the air out of car tyres outside the ECW Arena. Coraluzzo said they had specifically targeted one person's vehicle over a private dispute.

* In early 1994, Shane Douglas appeared on Mike Tenay's radio show to refute allegations that he had intentionally missed an independent event in Michigan. After Douglas went off-air, Coraluzzo phoned in and accused Douglas of frequently missing events across the country. Douglas angrily denied the allegations and challenged Coraluzzo to produce evidence.

* When the tournament was announced, Coraluzzo said he would have nothing to do with it, and said it was not authorised by the board. He later backtracked on this story.

* The 13 August issue of the *Pro Wrestling Torch* reported that ECW was considering a change of name that would involve keeping the same initials. At this point Heyman had privately discussed adopting the term 'Extreme' with Gordon.

* All major parties involved have said the arrangement was that Douglas would win the title and then lose the belt on another NWA promoter's show, most likely to Chris Benoit.

* Future Philadelphia NBC sportscaster John Clark (a partner in Legends of Wrestling) became aware of plans for a double-cross and informed Coraluzzo. He later told the *Wrestling Observer*'s Dave Meltzer that Coraluzzo either did not believe him, or chose to act as a 'martyr' for the NWA.

* Terry Funk did not appear as scheduled at the show, with fans told he had missed his flight. He did not appear in ECW again

until February 1995. Gordon later said Funk had tired of Paul Heyman's notoriously disorganised travel arrangements and left the company. At the time, one school of thought said Funk was aware of plans for the double-cross and intentionally missed the show; another theory said he only decided to leave permanently after the double-cross took place. Funk did not address the issue of his absence in his 2005 autobiography *More Than Just Hardcore*, but criticised the double-cross while speaking for the *Forever Hardcore* documentary.

* Following the double-cross, Gordon told Coraluzzo the incident was an angle to establish Douglas' character and that they wanted the storyline to involve the NWA forcing him to defend the title. Both men say Coraluzzo then took two takes to give his promo, though this was later exaggerated to 'many takes' by Coraluzzo-detractors.

* Between the tournament and the airing of the TV show, Coraluzzo told the *Pro Wrestling Torch* that "I was double-crossed. I went there as a team player with the NWA and with all that happened before, I thought this would wipe the slate clean. I was sincere and wasn't working anyone." Gordon refused to comment.

* The following week, Gordon told the *Torch* that Coraluzzo had verbally attacked ECW after the tournament was announced. "As a result, I had to figure a way to extricate ourselves and leave the NWA... Yes, this was a swerve. This guy had an obsession with this promotion for 18 months. He was begging for it. I have no regrets about the way the situation was handled."

* Shane Douglas appeared on the 4 September editions of Mike Tenay and John Arezzi's radio shows, which were traditionally based on covering wrestling legitimately, with wrestler interviews not being 'in character'. On both shows, Douglas claimed he had spontaneously decided to thrown the belt away, and that there was no prior arrangement with Gordon or Heyman.

* Heyman appeared later on the same edition of Arezzi's show, unaware of Douglas' comments, and said the incident was planned well in advance.

* Speaking in an interview with RF Video four years later, Coraluzzo said that he was aware in advance that the double-cross would take place, but that NWA lawyer Bob Trobich had advised he could not take pre-emptive action. Coraluzzo added that he decided to go ahead as if he were unaware of the plan and attempt to position himself favourably with the media after the event.

* In the 2005 *Forever Hardcore* DVD, Douglas claimed that only he and Heyman had prior knowledge of the double-cross, that Heyman left the final decision up to him, and that he was not certain he would go ahead with it until the moment. Speaking in the same documentary, Gordon said he was also involved in the planning.

The finish of the 1997 Survivor Series was the most famous double-cross in wrestling history, but the events of 27 August 1994 were in some ways even stranger. It is clear that a feud between Gordon and Coraluzzo led to Gordon, Douglas and Heyman plotting a double-cross. It seems extremely likely that the 'secret' was so poorly kept that Coraluzzo knew it was coming, yet willingly played the victim role. The man being double-crossed knew it was coming; the men doing the double-cross didn't know he knew. And following the event, even years later, it seems nobody could keep their stories straight.

As much as the NWA title double-cross was the birth of Extreme Championship Wrestling, a promotion built around rejecting the traditional rules of wrestling (both in and out of the ring), its roots lay in a series of events that were dishonest, sleazy, unprofessional and, in the world of pro wrestling, business as usual.

8: Extreme expansion

"It's simple: Accentuate the positives. Hide the negatives."
(Paul Heyman, The Rise And Fall of ECW*)*

Perhaps the biggest irony of the double-cross was that the rejection of the National Wrestling Alliance was immediately followed by ECW's first steps to national expansion. On 23 September the promotion debuted in Florida and drew better than expected thanks largely to local promotion by Dory Funk Jr; in a poor piece of timing, the shows came several days *before* ECW TV's delayed debut on the Florida-based Sunshine cable network. This TV expansion was followed in January by a slot on New York's MSG network, making it viable to run live shows in the market (at this point ECW had only run a small show in upstate Yonkers).

The new TV outlets were costing "several thousand dollars a week" according to Gordon, which makes it virtually certain the expansion was not self-financing. The home videos were contributing to costs, but by Gordon's estimates of 300-400 sales per tape, the revenue for 1994 would have been something in the region of $50,000 (before paying production and distribution costs). To give an idea of the company's financial state, ECW sold around 7,000 tickets between the Florida debut and the end of the year. If you take the ticket pricing structure of the time ($25 ringside, $12 general admission), add the tape sales, and allow a generous $10 per head in merchandise sales (the company's all time record for one show, years later, was just under $19 a head), ECW is unlikely to have been grossing much more than $15,000 a week. Once you take into consideration arena hire, advertising, television airtime costs, TV production costs, home video costs and payoffs to talent, it is difficult at the least to see how the company could have been even close to profitable.

At first sight it would therefore seem very strange that it was right at this time that the company stopped producing home videos. However, there was some logic to the move; the poorly-attended TV tapings at the Arena were dropped and footage was now taken from the main shows. This was a major factor in the growth of viewer interest in the TV (among both broadcast viewers and tape trader customers) with the show consisting almost entirely of competitive 'star vs star' matches, a year before the launch of *Nitro* made this standard practice in WCW and the WWF. To keep the product fresh each week, and to allow some ECW Arena matches to be exclusive to the live event, dedicated television tapings were held at the Hamburg Fieldhouse, home of the WWF's secondary television show *Championship Wrestling* in the 1970s and 80s. Competing at the venue was of particular significance to childhood viewer Mick Foley (Cactus Jack) who was now one half of the tag champions, having won the match against Public Enemy where Terry Funk's no-show left him to pick Mikey Whipwreck as his unlikely partner.

(Funk would make a shock return in February in a particularly creative angle. Cactus wrestled DC Drake, who was wheeled to the ring in a box. During the match, Sandman came out of the box and attacked Cactus, before being forced back into the box and covered with a blanket. He then staggered back into the ring where Cactus pulled off the blanket... and found Funk, wearing identical clothing to Sandman.)

Having left WCW, Cactus' first match as an ECW regular probably left him with less fond memories of the Hamburg venue after Sabu took several attempts to smash a bottle over his head to win the pair's rematch; Sabu didn't get off lightly. having broken several ribs when a missed Asaisault left him crashing stomach-first to the guard rail. While not quite in the same league, Tommy Dreamer had his own Hamburg horror story: at a December event a booking quirk meant he competed in three singles matches, a tag bout, a six-man tag and a battle royal!

Dreamer was also a part of arguably the most memorable angle in the history of the company during this period. At the tapings held the day after the NWA tournament, he took on Sandman in a match where the loser would be caned ten times. Woman interfered to give Sandman the win, which prompted Gordon to say that Dreamer did not have to take the cane shots because of the interference. Dreamer demanded to take his punishment like a man and refused to quit, even breaking out the line "Thank you sir, may I have another?", adapted from *National Lampoon's Animal House*. The legitimate brutality of the shots, which left even the Philadelphia hardcores wincing, was effectively the turning point in Dreamer being accepted as a 'hardcore' wrestler.

But there was more to come. Dreamer having refused to give up, the pair were rematched in an I Quit bout. It ended with Sandman apparently having a cigarette knocked into his eye and being taken to the dressing room while Tod Gordon screamed for a doctor. The fact that this aired on television should have alerted viewers it was part of the show, but a combination of extremely credible reactions, then-rare reality (the camera going inside the dressing room, heels and faces appearing together, real names being used), internet followers being fed 'inside information' from Gordon to hint that it was a stunt gone wrong, and Sandman staying out of public view, meant a surprising number of dedicated followers believed what they saw. As Raven put it in *Forever Hardcore*, "Those are the best fans. They think they know so much, so they are the easiest to fool." (Among those who found the incident realistic were management at the Sunshine Network, who refused to air the episode, causing the previously mentioned delay in the TV show's Florida debut.)

Five weeks later at the second November to Remember show, after Dreamer beat former Sandman nemesis Tommy Cairo, Sandman came to the ring for a retirement ceremony, wearing sunglasses, an eye patch and, uncharacteristically, a suit. As Dreamer turned his back during a tearful speech, Sandman removed his glasses and eye patch and picked up his cane, prompting one of the strangest reactions ever seen in a wrestling audience. The fans gasped, then began cheering; not so much because of the storyline (in which the villain was about to betray and attack the hero), but more for the simple fact that they had been fooled. They realised that, for a few brief weeks, they had experienced something that had they had lost in the cartoonish worlds of the mainstream promotions: the feeling of legitimately believing in a fictional product.

The idea of appealing to the 'smart fans' by creating a mysterious middle ground between wrestling storylines and real life was never stronger than with the angles and actions of Shane Douglas. After the NWA tournament he aligned himself on screen with Doink the Clown, perhaps the ultimate symbol of the 'WWF circus', who now appeared under the character of Borne Again. The concept was that Matt Borne, the wrestler who portrayed Doink in the WWF, had been driven insane by the gimmick and no longer knew where Borne ended and Doink began. He would appear with only one side of his face covered in the traditional clown paint, and would assault opponents after the bell, forcing them to wear the infamous green-haired wig. The character was clearly complete fiction, yet to fans who despised the Doink character and all it stood for, it was a perfectly plausible concept. Sadly Borne left the company after a series of no-shows before the character could be further developed.

Douglas was also involved in a less-subtle appeal to the fans' views of the wrestling world. Opening match wrestler Chad Austin grabbed the microphone at a show and began praising Smoky Mountain Wrestling, the southern promotion run by Jim Cornette which offered a product ECW fans saw as symbolic of outdated traditional wrestling. Douglas hit the ring, beat him repeatedly, and forced him to proclaim ECW as superior. And this wasn't the only reference Douglas made to other promotions. While feuding with Ron Simmons and Too Cold Scorpio, he declared he would bring in Steve Austin (regarded by the hardcore fans as the most under-appreciated wrestler in WCW) as his partner. What was billed on television as Douglas performing the impossible came about in reality through an odd series of events. The show earlier in the year with Eaton and Anderson had been named When Worlds Collide on the home video. WCW used the same title when it produced a PPV featuring the Mexican AAA group in November of 1994. ECW threatened legal action but dropped the case in return for being allowed to book Austin for the night. In the event, Austin was injured and replaced by Brian Pillman.

During this time, Douglas made the news for two lengthy performances with very different reactions. On the first show of 1995, he defended the title against Tully Blanchard (who was brought in to symbolise the Ric Flair style of 'old school' wrestler) in what was announced as a 60 minute draw. Accounts vary as to whether it was actually 43 or 51 minutes, but either way it didn't end a moment too soon for the fans. While there was an argument the bloodthirsty regulars didn't appreciate a mat-based match, most on hand claimed it was simply a dull match. Fans were hardly subtle about their dislike for the bout, chanting "Who booked this crap?", "Somebody do the job" and "We want bingo", with some spectators literally turning their backs on the contest. When the match was followed by a main event that went just five minutes, fans left in a foul mood, particularly as this was the first Arena show since the building stopped running Saturday night bingo, meaning there was no logistical need for such a short main event.

But the following month Douglas was more than redeemed by what was then a groundbreaking piece of wrestling television. Years before Triple H would ramble for 20 minutes at a time, the hour-long ECW TV show opened with a 30 minute Shane Douglas sit-down promo where the line between character and reality was blurry at best. At this point, other than Bob Barnett's *Looking For Mr Gilbert* video, the now-familiar shoot interview home video was unheard of. This was bordering on a shoot interview *during the show itself*, yet done in a way that did not question wrestling as a legitimate contest in which Douglas tried to out-wrestle his opponents.

The beauty of this approach (which fell by the wayside when it was bastardised by the likes of Vince Russo) was that it was used for the right person, in the right place, at the right time. And in many ways, that was the beauty of ECW booking at its pinnacle: people were used in the way that made best use of their abilities. So while Douglas talked for 30 minutes, 911 did not grab the microphone, claim he was deviating from the script, call himself 'Big Al', and launch into a diatribe about how his character was being misused by the booker. Instead, he ran to the ring, chokeslammed somebody, and left. His list of victims now went beyond other wrestlers; at November to Remember, a guitarist named Michael Lawler played the national anthem and deliberately missed several notes, with the crowd's hostile reaction being satisfied by a chokeslam. A month later at Holiday Hell, Santa Claus tasted the move in an homage to the 1968 football incident. (This was three years before Steve Austin gave St Nick a stunner on *RAW*.)

But for all of Paul Heyman's creative genius, there were some things he couldn't control. And one of his most complex plans was about to come apart just as it hit its peak.

9: The Three Way Dance

"He just went out there, broke character, and told the truth. It was weird." (*Ted 'Rocco Rock' Petty on Paul Heyman*, Pro Wrestling Torch)

One of the myths of ECW history is that the term 'Three Way Dance' originated with Sabu vs Funk vs Douglas; in fact it did not come about until over a year later with a triangular tag match pitting Sabu & Tazmaniac vs Public Enemy vs Chris Benoit and Dean Malenko. While Heyman and Gordon clearly wanted to use the concept (an original plan had Eddy Guerrero and Art Barr taking part, fresh off their appearance at the AAA/WCW When Worlds Collide pay-per-view, the plan falling through with Barr's untimely death), this was not a case of throwing together a random set of wrestlers as is so often the case with today's imitators. Long before "three way" became wrestling shorthand for "the promoter booked an odd number of people for the show", the original ECW Three Way Dance would cap off storylines running back almost eight months.

Tensions began in August of 1994 when Rocco Rock began performing his 'Drive-by' (a 180 degree flip into a splash, properly titled a senton) through a table, with Joey Styles on commentary noting it as a move from Sabu's repertoire. When Rock began using tables in more spectacular ways (the first ever 'Drive-by' through *two* tables was considered a jaw-dropping move at the time), Styles again referred to Sabu, and when Rock prepared to dive from the ECW Arena stage onto Mikey Whipwreck (who lay on a table), it proved too much. Sabu ran from the locker-room and shoved Rock from the platform.

Meanwhile, Malenko was billed as a henchman of Jason (Knight, now the TV champion), and would attack and injure his opponents after each match with what was billed as 'shooter' techniques: joint-based submission holds. Tazmaniac was the first person to avoid such a fate, reversing an armlock. As he was still portraying the long-haired, silent wildman character, this was unexpected by most viewers, who were unaware of his amateur background.

And the third strand of the rivalry came when a much-anticipated Benoit vs Sabu match at November to Remember ended in barely a minute after a Benoit suplex went off-course and Sabu landed directly on his head and fractured his neck. Amusingly or sickeningly (depending on your attitude), in-ring 'aggressor' Benoit drove Sabu to the hospital and made repeated enquiries in the following days about his progress, while Sabu's manager Paul E Dangerously quickly reverted to promoter mode and began coming up with ideas to market Benoit on the back of the incident. Repackaging Benoit as 'The Crippler', Heyman booked a series of incidents where opponents would apparently suffer serious injuries; what made it particularly effective was that it was never entirely clear whether Benoit's character was intentionally hurting opponents, or if it was merely the unavoidable result of a no-nonsense style.

Long-time Sabu followers were hardly surprised when he took little notice of conventional medical wisdom and returned to the ring two weeks later to team with Taz against Dean and Joe Malenko. (Ironically, despite his enthusiasm to get back in action, Sabu was reported to be less happy about working as part of a regular team, reasoning that his crazed character would be unlikely to stand patiently at ringside awaiting a legal tag. The obvious caveat to this story is that ECW referees were hardly noted for their insistence on traditional tag conventions, with tornado-style multi-man brawls the usual course of business.) The match ended with what was becoming firmly established as the ECW trademark: a series of run-ins bringing together a variety of feuds. Jason attacked Paul E; the Pitbulls ran out to defend Jason; 911 chokeslammed the Pitbulls; Public Enemy came out to get revenge on Sabu; both Sabu and Dangerously went through tables.

Malenko and Benoit's union began informally in an 'extreme warfare' match (a version of the WWF's Royal Rumble bout) when they teamed to injure Ron Simmons, and became official when they interfered together to help Public Enemy beat Sabu and Taz on the final ECW Arena show of 1994. As was often the case with classic Heyman booking, two storylines then overlapped: Benoit and

Malenko then formed an alliance with Shane Douglas, who put together this 'Triple Threat' group in response to his feud with Tully Blanchard (playing off Blanchard's role in the 1980s Four Horsemen stable).

With table-breaking at the centre of the storyline, it was a logical enough choice that the Public Enemy-Sabu/Tazmaniac rematch should be a 'double tables' match, won only when one team put both opponents through tables. The match headlined the 4 February 1995 Arena show, which marked the first of Tom Misnik's internet conventions. A disputed finish (the referee missing what should have been a Public Enemy win) led to new tag champions, but the night's major incident came after the bout: as Sabu prepared to legdrop Rocco Rock through a table, Benoit ran out, climbed to the top rope, and powerbombed Sabu straight onto Rock, both men crashing through the furniture. While this move would probably now get you a two count in the opening match of most indy shows, at the time it was so spectacular that for several months hardcore fans would refer to it simply as 'the spot'.

Two weeks later, Rock appeared for a ringside interview in a wheelchair, prompting Benoit to come out and run the chair straight into a crowd barrier. After Benoit and Malenko took the tag titles from Sabu and Tazmaniac later that night, Public Enemy ran out (with Rock's clothes bloodied up to show the damage from the chair incident) and all six men brawled to the back. Public Enemy issued the inevitable challenge on television and the Three Way Dance was scheduled for 8 April. So detailed was the build-up that a recap of the feud took up seventeen minutes of the final television show before the event, and it was the first show where videotape orders (now being handled by bootleg trader Rob Feinstein) were accepted before the show even happened.

So you can probably see why people weren't too impressed when Sabu didn't turn up.

In late 1994, it became widely known that both WCW and WWF had shown interest in signing him to a full-time contract (WWF having given him tryout matches the previous year against Owen Hart and Scott Taylor, now known as Scotty 2 Hotty). At one point it was even rumoured that ECW had responded by giving him a guaranteed weekly contract, though this was not the case. Eventually he settled on a deal with New Japan Pro Wrestling that gave him regular tours, while leaving him free to work ECW and other independent dates when he didn't have Japanese bookings.

When Sabu agreed to work the Three Way Dance show, he did not have a Japanese date booked for 8 April; indeed, New Japan was not running a tour at the time. However, Sabu then agreed to work on a one-off date for Heisei Ishingun (a supposed independent company which was actually run by New Japan to create an 'inter-promotional' feud), apparently under the assumption he could make both shows because of the time difference. When it became clear no connecting flight existed to make this possible, Sabu had to make a choice.

To the ECW fans, it should have been obvious: there was no question that the heavily-hyped Three Way Dance was more important (this view being reinforced when the Japan date turned out to be a second-match double countout with mid-carder Gedo). But to Sabu, job security was the priority. While his ECW payoffs were respectable, he was working barely twice a month for the group, while New Japan offered regular dates for guaranteed money; he claimed New Japan paid him his weekly touring salary for the April trip, even though he worked a single date. If he had to upset one employer, it would have to be ECW rather than New Japan. Although his in-ring character was a crazed lunatic, the thirty-year old had revealed more civilised concerns in a *Pro Wrestling Torch* interview the previous summer:

"If they can't give me more matches per month or more money... I'm not trying to pressure them, but I'm not getting any younger and neither is my mother. I want to take care of my mother better. So the only way I can do that is to make more money."

While those who recognised the realities of the wrestling business would conclude Sabu made the best decision for his circumstances, his handling left plenty to be desired. He still claimed to be able to make both dates, even one week before the show when Heyman asked him to make a final decision so that he could put together the TV show without having to risk what would be seen as false-advertising. While Heyman must presumably have been suspicious, it probably wasn't until he phoned two days before the event and got an answerphone message from Sabu saying he'd left for Japan that it became clear he would not be making the date. (The pair dispute if or when Sabu specifically said he could not appear for ECW, though both agree Heyman was right to be expecting the appearance when he put together the TV show.)

Heyman's own handling of the problem on the night of the event was widely praised, though it arguably only stood out because it took place in the traditionally sleazy and dishonest world of pro wrestling promotion. Before the show started, he addressed the crowd, explained what he knew of the situation, and told fans they could watch the first half of the show and then leave during intermission with a full refund. (This became standard ECW policy and was in stark contrast to WWF and WCW whose policy on no-shows, whether unavoidable problem or intentional fraudulent advertising, was a flat 'tough luck'.) In a characteristic display of psychology, Heyman did not specifically criticise Sabu, instead saying he was disappointed in him, announced he was indefinitely suspended (the independent contractor equivalent of a firing), said he had found a replacement (who turned out to be Rick Steiner) and invited the crowd to make their own minds up.

The crowd's conclusion on the dilemma of whether to support the individual wrestler or the promotion came almost instantly and took the form of just two words repeated at length:

"FUCK SABU!"

10: A storied summer

"Stop the excitement: I'm a public official!" (Bill Alfonso)

The departure of Sabu was, understandably, a hot talking point among hardcore fans and the insider wrestling media. Yet the irony is that it came just one day after a barely-publicised event that was arguably among the most important in ECW's history. On 7 April 1995, papers were filed with the State of New York to set up HHG Corp. Until this point, the promotion had been run by a Philadelphia company (Eastern Championship Wrestling) set up on 30 January 1992 and owned solely by Gordon. The new HHG Corp took over the promotion and, for simplicity, any future references to 'ECW' as a business in this book should be taken as referring to HHG Corp.

As a private business, the full ownership details of ECW during this period did not have to be made public, so it is difficult to be certain about timelines. If Tod Gordon's accounts are accurate, Heyman worked without pay from September 1993 and was instead rewarded with a 49% partnership deal. As part of the HHG formation, Heyman bought out Gordon's share of the promotion by paying off the company's outstanding debts (probably with money provided by Heyman's father). Gordon left the company in 1997 claiming to have walked away with at least enough money to cover his losses since starting the promotion, which reportedly involved taking out a second mortgage at one point.

What is certain is that Heyman was the registered chief executive officer of HHG Corp, which was legally registered to the family address in Scarsdale, New York. Also listed on the company filing was his lawyer father Richard S Heyman (in an administrative role that was the US equivalent to a company secretary), in time a major financial contributor to the company. Given these details, it hardly seems an unreasonable assumption that HHG referred to Heyman, Heyman and Gordon.

While HHG began clearing debts, and giving the promotion a legal base for expansion, it certainly had teething problems. On the first set of shows organised without Gordon in control, wrestlers reported they had been booked on last-minute flights that cost the company up to four times the usual rates, while others arrived to find hotel rooms had not been booked as expected. Such transport problems would be a familiar complaint among wrestlers throughout the next few years.

Similar problems were affecting the company's television syndication, with some delays caused by moving the duplication and distribution of tapes in-house. (This became the responsibility of the Stonecutter group, headed by Steve Karel, who would go on to take many roles in the company. Stonecutter also began making deals to authorise the use of popular rock songs on the TV show and home video, a part of the product's appeal to its intended MTV-style audience that cannot be overstated.) That's not to say the television stations themselves were blameless: at one stage the MSG network delayed the airing of one show by three days, meaning that the final hype for an ECW Arena show aired the day *after* the event.

Despite the problems, the company continued to expand its network, debuting on television in Ohio, though oddly the company would not run live shows there for three years. On its next trip to Florida, crowds were up by around 50%. There were even plans to run an outdoor show in Scranton, Pennsylvania's Lackawanna Stadium with hopes to draw around 15,000 for a Terry Funk vs Cactus Jack match with a fire-related stipulation. (The event fell through when stadium owners demanded a $9,500 fee to cover the turf before the ring and seats could be set up.)

Driving the business expansion was perhaps the most tightly booked series of live events and television shows that any company has ever put together. The Raven vs Tommy Dreamer feud is detailed in full in a later chapter, and this was just one aspect of the company's product at the time, in which many different storylines and feuds would become entangled to produce true non-stop action. One ECW Arena show alone, Hardcore Heaven, featured two debuts, two turns, five chokeslams, a reversed decision by a heel referee, a Taipei death match, a firing, a cage match, an in-ring celebration by fifty fans, and a match involving a water melon and a croquet mallet!

Though it was not always the main event, the ECW title remained protected as a focal point of the company; the opening montage of the show would always conclude with the reigning champion. And it was perhaps symbolic that the renegade, no-frills promotion should get a new champion to match, one who had famously declared himself, and the promotion, to be "politically incorrect, and damn proud of it". On 8 April, Douglas successfully defended the title against Sandman after Woman turned on her charge. But in a rematch a week later it proved to be a doublecross by the dastardly vixen as she helped Sandman begin what, at the time, seemed the most unlikely of title reigns; little did fans know what was in store later in the year. Meanwhile Douglas' follow-up storyline virtually wrote itself: he negotiated with the WWF and signed a deal, with his decision to wear a *Monday Night RAW* t-shirt in the ECW Arena ring perhaps the most villainous action imaginable.

Except, that is, enforcing the rules. While it is something of a myth that ECW never did disqualifications (in 1995 alone, 16 matches ended this way), it was certainly true that the prevailing attitude to matches was 'anything goes'. By 13 May, Raven and Dreamer's matches had seen widespread interference and everything from hairspray to cheesegraters being used without repercussions from officials. But on that date, Douglas came out at the start of a Raven & Steve Richards vs Dreamer & Mikey Whipwreck match and announced that the Pennsylvania State Athletic Commission had appointed a special referee for the match. In a link with Douglas' own storyline, it was occasional WWF official Bill Alfonso, who went on to disqualify Dreamer for, of all things, using a closed fist. So angry were the fans that it is reported some actually waited outside the arena following the show in hope of getting their hands on Alfonso.

In the following months, Alfonso was effectively the company's lead heel. He overturned an apparent Cactus Jack ECW title win (he had won a barbed wire match by knocking Sandman out for the count of ten, but Alfonso ruled the title couldn't change hands this way), forced both Dreamer and Whipwreck to wrestle when injured rather than be replaced in their matches, and even insisted Whipwreck receive a full ten strokes of the cane from Sandman thanks to a match stipulation; after seven brutal strokes, Whipwreck had been placed on a stretcher. (This angle, accompanied by orgasmic screams of delight by Woman, was edited from the TV show by affiliates on the Prime Network, while Heyman pulled the show from

Florida's Sunshine Network rather than edit it. The resulting standoff, coupled with Sunshine's demands that ECW doubled the $750 it paid the network to air the show each week, led to the loss of TV in Florida. This effectively cost ECW its second biggest market, and the company did not run another show in Florida for two years.) When a show was delayed by more than an hour because of ring problems, Alfonso took the blame, claiming to have demanded the promotion use a 20 foot square ring as in the WWF. Long before the evil authority figure became a success with Eric Bischoff and Vince McMahon (and a tired cliché with the countless imitators), Alfonso served to embody everything ECW fans hated, from inconclusive finishes to petty authority.

That's not to say the finer points of the wrestling rulebook were in effect throughout the card. One of ECW's most notorious feuds involved The Bad Breed, Axl and Ian Rotten. After losing a match to The Pitbulls where the defeated team was forced to split, they began a rivalry based on the logic that "If you can't join them, beat them." Their matches became progressively more violent, meeting in a barbed wire baseball bat match, a strap match, a hair vs hair contest, a barbed wire baseball bat match with the addition of a chair wrapped in barbed wire, and a taped fist match. After all this, they were willing to put their differences aside for a bout with Public Enemy, but predictably Alfonso insisted they uphold their stipulation to never team again. (The fans' displeasure was soon forgotten when the Smoky Mountain Wrestling team of New Jack and Mustafa, The Gangstas, made a surprise appearance and attacked Public Enemy). The Rottens instead decided to settle their feud with a Taipei Death match in which both men had broken glass taped to their fists (the stip borrowed from the Jean Claude Van Damme film *Bloodsport*). Barely a minute had passed before Alfonso declared the match over because of a trickle of blood, but fortunately for gore-lovers he was immediately distracted by a Gangstas-Public Enemy brawl which had spilled out from the dressing room. Gordon declared the match back on and, thanks to a bag of thumbtacks, Axl took the win. While there are many arguments against this style of wrestling, particularly its growth to main event status among so many independent shows today, it's worth remembering that not only was it just a small part of

ECW's appeal, but it was far more effective, coming at a time when such matches were usually only seen on videotapes imported from Japan's FMW and W*ING promotions. Indeed, one of the main purposes of these bouts, aside from satisfying the bloodthirsty, was to provide selling points for the home videos of ECW Arena shows, these matches clearly being unsuitable for broadcast on TV.

If blood and guts wasn't your cup of tea, on the same show you could watch Dean Malenko and Eddy Guerrero putting together a series of matches that would be spoken about in the same tones as Brisco-Funk or Flair-Steamboat. Their final bout is the best known, but their first ECW contest (a thirty minute draw) is arguably the most stylistically influential US match of its time, at least in terms of independent wrestling. Guerrero was already a star within the Hispanic audience thanks to AAA's show on Galavision, but this match brought together New Japan junior-heavyweight style with lucha techniques to produce the blueprint for 'modern' American wrestling. The bout's finishing sequence, a series of reversed pin attempts, was not new (it had appeared in similar form in an Owen Hart-Danny Collins match in England four years earlier to give one example), but thanks to this match it is now used for a guaranteed pop on indy shows across the Western Hemisphere; nobody could actually explain *why* they cheer it today, it's just the done thing. What is sadly forgotten by the imitators is that in Malenko-Guerrero it played a logical part in the contest, which put across the story that both men were evenly matched, and this was their final desperate attempt to take the victory before the time limit expired.

The theme of the rivalry being too close to call would underpin the feud, with the first two matches being thirty minute draws. The pair then went on the road for a series of three matches in two days, winning one apiece and the other going to a draw. They exchanged the TV title in Florida and New York, and also took one win apiece on other spot shows. In tag matches they took a pin apiece. (Crowds outside Philadelphia were not always so enamoured with their matches: the verbal complaints of one set of fans in Florida prompted Heyman to grab the microphone during a Guerrero/Taz vs Scorpio/Malenko match and proclaim "I'm sorry if you find a fine display of scientific wrestling boring, but I was wondering if you could peel your foreskin back so I could see your nose.") And memorably their final match, best of three falls, saw a double-pin in the deciding fall; nobody complained about the screwjob as the pair were lifted on the shoulders of other wrestlers and departed the ring with many in tears.

One reason for the emotion was another masterstroke by Heyman in manipulating his specific audience. In reality, Malenko, Guerrero and Chris Benoit had all been offered contracts by WCW (which was attempting to expand its roster as it launched *Monday Nitro* to go head to head with the WWF) and, having confirmed they could continue touring with New Japan (thanks to the company's relationship with WCW), they decided to accept the deal as a group. While Heyman on record refused to call this anything more than good business by WCW, the story floating among ECW fans was that WCW had persuaded New Japan to threaten the three that they would lose their Japanese dates if they did not accept the deal. For those who understood the bigger picture, it would have been clear that ECW was a secondary job for the trio behind their Japan commitments (indeed, Benoit had been given WWF tryout matches that summer, but turned down a job as it would have meant an end to his New Japan tours). But to ECW fans, WCW was painted as a bigger heel than any company villain, and many fans were convinced the trio would be back the moment their initial 90-day contractual period ended; in the event, they stayed in WCW for more than four years. Speaking in the ECW Arena, Heyman's comment "Of course you know, this means war!" received a resounding response and became yet another popular t-shirt slogan.

But while some wrestlers came and went, you were guaranteed one thing in the summer of 1995: 911 would continue chokeslamming anyone who met with the crowd's disapproval. 'Jungle' Jim Steele, a former WCW opening match performer whose muscular physique outshone his in-ring ability, received a record five choke slams. (Three years later he returned under his All Japan name of Wolf Hawkfield and was accepted by the crowd.) In one incident, lower-card wrestler Chad Austin began deliberately, but subtly missing moves until the unsuspecting crowd began to berate him, leading to chokeslams for he, his partner and both opponents. A New York ring announcer 'mistakenly' introduced him as "991", earning a chokeslam. Tape trader Rob Feinstein, who, rightly or wrongly, received the blame for delays with shipping the company's home videos, met the same fate, as did colleague Doug Gentry, who appeared as the New Jersey Devil (Philadelphia's bitter rival in ice hockey). But Bill Alfonso evaded the move time and time again, even going as far as to ban the chokeslam.

Until 16 September 1995 and *that* match.

Some people dispute the case that Raven & Steve Richards vs The Pitbulls in a best-of-three-falls double dog-collar bout is the greatest match in ECW history. They have the right to that opinion, but in throwing around terms such as 'moveset', 'smoke and mirrors' and 'execution', they miss the point of ECW and wrestling as a whole. The idea is not to produce a performance that rates highly on some supposedly objective and scientific scale. The idea is to engage the audience and manipulate their emotions.

This match was not just a random selection of crazy moves, bleeding, chairshots and table demolition (though it certainly had its share). Viewed in isolation, its true effect cannot be appreciated. But to those who had been following ECW throughout the year, it was the ultimate in roller-coaster storytelling.

After two falls of general chaos, the crowd's interest continued to rise as the four brawled around the building (where one Pitbull had a planned exchange of blows with Gentry and a friend, both dressed as Raven, in a spot missed by the cameras). Back at ringside, Raven legdropped Pitbull 2 through two tables, causing him to be taken away on a stretcher. Tommy Dreamer came out and inserted himself into the match and, as Francine and Beulah began fighting, he DDTed Raven and pinned him for the 'first' time, a moment months in the making. Except it didn't count, because Bill Alfonso (reasonably enough) pointed out that Dreamer was not the legal man, prompting Tod Gordon to begin brawling with Alfonso. Big Dick Dudley (who had saved Alfonso from 911 on several occasions) took advantage of the distraction to come to the ring and chokeslam Dreamer. After Gordon demanded Dudley be suspended for the move, Alfonso made the mistake of announcing that the move was legal for one night only. What happened next was as predictable as a Hulk Hogan comeback, and no less effective. 911 hit the ring (with his music playing) and *finally* chokeslammed Alfonso to a rapturous reception. All that remained was for Pitbull 2 to return to the ring and set up a double superbomb on both Raven and Richards leading directly to the pin, the title change, and another momentous pop. This was not something that could be analysed on a five star scale. This was six months of foreplay culminating in a triple orgasm. This was ECW.

And Steve Austin was backstage.

11 : Fire and pizazz

"The guys that are backstage [in ECW] know that the people are going to get into it. They're not looking down at the people thinking they're marks in any way, shape or form." (Steve Austin, Pro Wrestling Torch *yearbook)*

To say that the man who would become the biggest draw in the history of the business made his name in ECW would be ridiculous; a pro for six years, Steve Austin been touted as a future superstar from virtually the first day he wrestled in public. But despite a four year spell in WCW including a successful run with Brian Pillman as the Hollywood Blondes, perhaps the company's last great tag team, he was surplus to requirements in the Hulk Hogan era. Former boss Eric Bischoff had even told him that his plain black trunks and boots look did not lend itself to storylines or merchandising opportunities and, while a competent talker, he was not known for delivering great promos. But when Steve Austin arrived in ECW, it soon became clear that careful scriptwriting was not necessary.

"The first lengthy interview I cut was six or seven minutes," he recalled in the 1995 *Pro Wrestling Torch* yearbook. "It was 4:30 in the morning by that time and I didn't even want to do that interview because I didn't have anything to talk about. [Heyman] just told me to go out there and talk."

And talk he did.

"A couple weeks ago, when Eric Bischoff told his secretary to tell her secretary to leave a message on my answering machine for me to call Eric Bischoff and then I called Eric Bischoff and he proceeded to fire me over the phone, I thought a big cloud was lifted off the career of Steve Austin. Because gone were the days when I'd go up to someone and say 'Hey, what about me and Sting? We got this big thing going, how 'bout the cage?' and someone says [in the voice of Dusty Rhodes] *'No baby, thath for thomebody elthe. We jutht gonna keep you right where you at right now.' Then I said 'Well what*

about me and Savage? I got this great idea: he comes in, he's got the Slim Jim deal, well hell, I got...' 'No Thteve. Thath for thomebody elthe, baby.' Then you go 'I got this great idea. I could do it with Hulk Hogan. I'm gonna be the Steve-a-maniac and we're gonna take this thing all the way! Because Hulk Hogan, Hulkamania was the biggest thing to ever come down the wrestling pike!' And they said 'No, that's not for you, brother. You can't do that. We're gonna keep you right where you are.'

"I said 'How about me and Brian get back together? The Hollywood Blondes! It was the best tag team to come along in ten years!' and they say 'No Steve, we need you in a singles role man. We need you to do this. We're gonna put the US title on you and then we're gonna take you here, and then you're the number one contender so then you get this world title shot...' Well all that shit never happened!

"So there I am, floundering along, there's nothing going my way, because the politics in WCW kept the biggest potential superstar in wrestling on the goddamn ground! What are you supposed to do? On one hand, they're paying you a bunch of money... they're paying ME a bunch of money. While on this hand they're saying 'Hey, go out and give Bagwell a hell of a match. Go out there with an 18-year-old German kid. Give him seven good minutes. Let the people see what he can do.'

"They say you are what you eat. In WCW, they didn't feed me nothing but garbage, so I let myself become garbage. I became complacent with everything they said. As long as big Ted kept sending in the cheques...maybe I wasn't happy with everything that was going on, but I became complacent.

"Then they send me to Japan... the big injury! Bischoff delivers the shot heard around the damn world: Steve Austin's out of the high-paying job. All of a sudden the phone starts ringing off the hook... it's ECW, it's the WWF, it's All Japan, it's New Japan, and all Steve Austin's gotta do is make a decision. Tod Gordon, whether he re-mortgaged his house one time, two times, maybe three times, came up with the right figure for Steve Austin to make a decision.

"I stroll into the ECW Arena: the biggest piece of crap I've ever seen. I broke in in a building called the Sportatorium in Dallas, Texas. Home of the world famous Von Erichs! Everybody who was *anybody set foot in the Dallas Sportatorium. For the last two years, all you've heard about anywhere in wrestling is the famous ECW Arena. Debut night, I roll in. You got the Sandman. You got Raven. You got the Pitbulls. You got Stevie Richards, you got the Public Enemy, you got the Gangstas, you got Mipey Whikrep... whatever the hell his name is! You got a bunch of damn MISFITS, running around thinking that they can actually wrestle. All I've seen in ECW is a bunch of violent crap and that's exactly what I'll call it 'cos that's exactly what it is. Steve Austin is here to wrestle. It's what I do best. It's what I do better than anyone in the world.*

"Dean Malenko, Eddy Guerrero, they got the big send-off. Tears were in everybody's eyes. It was a big deal. All Steve Austin got was a good swift kick in the ass as Bischoff hung up the phone and left me high and dry. There's no Hogans here. There's no Flairs here. There's not a Dusty Rhodes and there damn sure isn't an Eric Bischoff here. There's no-one that can hold back Steve Austin now.

"'Stunning'? Tossed it out the window. Never was meant to be. ECW's gonna find out first hand what Steve Austin can do. And I'm gonna show everyone here exactly what a true superstar is supposed to do, what a true superstar is supposed to be. Because no-one here can hold me back. Not Tod Gordon. Not Hulk Hogan. Not Eric Bischoff. Nobody. I'm gonna be the superstar that I always knew I could be, because there's no-one, no-one in ECW that can stop me."

Austin didn't stay long in ECW: he only worked two matches, losing a challenge to Mikey Whipwreck (who had miraculously won the title from Sandman), then pinning him in a three way dance, only to be pinned by Sandman (who thus regained the belt). But between his awakened ability behind the microphone, and whatever he picked up in the way of attitude from ECW (and Sandman's character in particular), Austin's spell in the company was the final step as he readied himself for greatness. For the next six months he floundered in the WWF under a pre-packaged, off-the-shelf 'Ringmaster' character before he won the King of The Ring tournament, looked at defeated opponent and religious advocate Jake Roberts, and delivered a spontaneous promo with a throwaway line about "Austin 3:16". The rest was history.

But the title of ECW's best interview belonged elsewhere. After turning heel, Cactus Jack delivered one of the greatest runs of promos ever seen in the business. Except these were not merely the storyline comments of Cactus Jack: they were largely the comments of Mick Foley. Explaining his turn as being a reaction against the hardcore fans, his weekly addresses were a reality-driven attack at ECW's audiences and what they demanded of their performers. Full transcripts of the promos appear in Foley's *Have A Nice Day*, but among the highlights were:

"Somebody had taken the time and the effort and the thought to make a sign that said, 'Cane Dewey'. And I saw other people around, as every moment in my life stopped and focused in on that sign and the pain that shot through my body became a distant memory, replaced by a thought which will be embedded in my skull until my dying day. Cane Dewey. Cane Dewey. Dewey Foley is a three-year-old little boy, you sick sons of bitches!"

(After seeing the *20/20* expose of wrestling in 1985.) *"That night I went to bed not with visions of sugarplums dancing through my head but of broken bones, of battered bodies and bloody corpses, saying to myself, 'If it's the last thing I do, if I have to hold myself up for a human sacrifice, the world will respect professional wrestling'... Professional wrestling will never be respected, no matter how many teeth I lose, no matter how many ears I lose, no matter how many brain cells have to die. And so it comes down to the point where it's just not worth it... Never in my sickest dreams did I imagine that there would be other wrestlers taking dives onto concrete floors, committing human suicide on my behalf, like I'm the patron saint of all the sick sons of bitches."*

"How many of you have gone up to Dynamite Kid and said, 'Kid, thanks for the dives on to the concrete floor. Sorry to hear you don't have a pot to piss in, or a window to throw it out of, but thanks for the memories.' You see, Tommy Dreamer, the problem with being hardcore is that, by the very nature of the name, we give: of ourselves, of our bodies, of our hearts, and of our souls, and for each

one of us who gives, there's bloodthirsty, lowlife fans out there only willing to take. How many of you shed a tear for Eddie Gilbert and, if you did, was it not just to feel sorry for yourselves that you won't get to see Eddie showered in blood anymore?"

Foley later wrote that he followed Michael Hayes' advice that an effective heel must believe what he says (whether in reality or merely character), but these interviews proved that a heel promo can be even more effective when the audience dislikes the message but knows it is true. The effect by which viewers would applaud the 'genius' of the interviews, while becoming uncomfortable as they recognised the truth of the message, may have been bizarre by traditional wrestling standards, but they achieved the most basic point of professional wrestling: stirring emotion in the fans and retaining their attention.

But as much as the fans thought they understood what Foley was doing and recognised it as a part of the show (albeit an unorthodox technique), he retained control of the crowd. While the smart fans would mock a heel who wore an opposing sports team's shirt as displaying 'cheap heat', Foley's home-made shirts proclaiming his love for Bischoff or WCW's cartoonish Dungeon of Doom stable provoked the desired response. In a match with rookie El Puerto Ricano, he teased delivering his trademark elbowdrop to the concrete floor, but instead slapped on a headlock.

And kept it there.

For several minutes.

He repeated the move in his next ECW Arena appearance, against Tommy Dreamer, following up by throwing a single punch, attempting to have the match stopped because his hand was injured, then asking to be counted out. The idea was to create a memorable image of ECW being the place that was so counter-culture that the most heelish move was to **not** viciously beat down the beloved hero. Unfortunately the night of 28 October 1995 would be remembered for something entirely unplanned.

After Dreamer pinned Cactus, a brawl broke out with cornermen Raven and Terry Funk. Funk brought out his trademark branding iron, lit on fire, while Cactus responded by setting light to a chair with a towel taped to it (his resthold-only offense was dropped when the occasion called for it). The tape caught fire, putting the flames out of control, and what was meant to be a teased swing at Funk wound up with the towel coming loose and breaking into pieces, one landing on Funk, setting him alight, and others going into the crowd. Meanwhile part of the ring had been soaked in kerosene in an earlier match (in which Rocco Rock set light to a table) and also caught fire. A security member used a fire extinguisher which turned out to be long past its best, causing as many problems with spectators choking as it solved by putting out the flames.

In hindsight, this was not the best time for the lights to go out.

The planned finish to the evening's show was that the lights would come back on to reveal Dreamer hanging from a balcony, symbolically 'crucified' by Raven. The controls for the building's lighting were backstage in a room without a clear view of the main arena, so the person responsible was unaware of the fire problems. The burned fan, Raymond Schweitzer went on to sue the company for $150,000 in damages but when the case came to trial, more than four years later, the jury rejected the claim. Among the main evidence influencing the verdict was that his hand had been over the guard rail (in the 'forbidden' ringside area) as he had grabbed the piece of towel caught on Funk, rather than being burned by the piece that went into the crowd. In the shorter term, the incident caused problems with the state athletic commission. While the meeting was held behind closed doors, it is believed that as there was no specific offence, the commission fined ECW's licensed promoter Ed Zohn on a technicality (not having a doctor on hand); Zohn left the company shortly afterwards. A member of the commission told the Connecticut Post that ECW repeatedly pushed the regulations, but there was little they could do about it with the industry largely deregulated: if they pulled a promoter's licence, the company would simply place somebody else in the role.

Had the Pennsylvania commission been as strict as its counterparts in states such as New York, where ringside mats were mandatory, one of the promotion's more entertaining gimmicks (and infamous chants) might never have been born. In a match with Hack

Myers (a cult figure whose every blow would be met by the crowd chanting his nickname "Shah!", while retaliatory strikes by his opponent earned the response "Shit!"), JT Smith caught his feet on the top rope during a dive to the outside, landing headfirst on the concrete and developing a swelling the size of an egg. Fortunately there was no permanent damage, and the incident was incorporated into his character, with him deliberately making mistakes and being greeted with playful chants of "You fucked up!" In years to come, this chant would be delivered disrespectfully at any sign of a missed move or injury, storyline or legitimate, causing understandable resentment on the part of wrestlers. Fans prided themselves on spotting 'injuries' that were merely part of the show, greeting the 'Damage Control' paramedics with an ironic rendition of an ambulance siren, but a portion of the fanbase appeared to celebrate legitimate injury with just as much excitement.

Coordination problems weren't the only result for the character of JT Smith. It appeared several wires had been crossed in his head, and he now believed himself to be a Philadelphia-style Italian-American. The difference between traditional wrestling ethnic stereotype and fresh visual comedy was that JT Smith was black. In time he was joined by the authentic Italian James Maritato (now christened Little Guido) and a giant counterpart logically enough named Big Guido. Smith paid homage to the Rocky Balboa statue. He ate pizza. He serenaded the crowd with *Fly Me To The Moon*. He did every Italian stereotype in the book, but with a post-modern ironic raised eyebrow. In later years, Tommy Rich (of Nashville, Italy), Tracey Smothers, and even Ulf Herman of Germany discovered their Italian roots.

Dubious as this heritage was, it was arguably more convincing than that of the Dudley clan. Originally made up of two wrestlers based on the Hanson brothers in *Slap Shot*, Dudley Dudley (apparently named in response to his inbred status) and Little Snot Dudley, new half-brothers were discovered amid stories that their father Big Daddy Dudley had been a travelling salesman who put himself about. Chubby Dudley, the result of a dalliance with an overweight lady, did little but stuff his face. Big Dick Dudley was so imposing that after he was hit by a truck the joke was that the truck came off worse. Dances with Dudley had resulted from a visit to an

Indian reservation where, wait for it, Big Daddy Dudley "poked a Hontas". Sign Guy Dudley never spoke, communicating through the written word. Buh Buh Ray Dudley (who originally debuted as Alfonso's bodyguard Mongo, a dig at *Nitro* commentator Steve McMichael) stuttered so badly that when he was invited to perform ring introductions at November to Remember, fans were assured "the sixty minute time limit will be strictly enforced". D-Von Dudley was the bible-thumping villain of the clan. And Spike was the runt of the litter. Nothing about the Dudley gimmick was sophisticated or intellectually challenging, but as a means of providing genuine humour and character for unproven lower-card talent, it more than did the trick.

The technique of never exposing a performer beyond his or her natural strengths was best displayed in an addition to the TV show that was so simplistically effective that it seems fresh even ten years later. Shows would now regularly end with a montage of promo clips to Dirk Dale's *Misirlou* (title theme of the recently released *Pulp Fiction*). Almost a microcosm of the promotion itself, the goal was to get as many points across and characters over as possible in half the time now allocated to an opening promo on *RAW*. Gifted talkers would deliver addresses of several minutes, others would hammer home their main point, one-note gimmicks would be struck in a variety of settings (Buh Buh's speech impediment manifested itself when his first driving lesson ended in repeated stalls), and Steve Williams kept his mouth shut and looked imposing.

The start of each show was just as important, as fan Kenny McBride describes:

You see, the thing about the ECW credits is that they tell you everything you need to know. Here's what you get:
<White noise>
To the opening beats of Closer *by Nine Inch Nails - a popular beat combo of the time - a screen appears from deep in the white noise, alternately flashing up letters in a vivid red and short clips of wrestlers doing things.*
E
Woman lights Sandman's cigarette
X

Cactus Jack hits Sandman with a trash can
T
911 chokeslams Doink
R
Paul E. Dangerously hits Sherri with his mobile phone
E
Taz hits a T-bone suplex on Dean Malenko
M
Cactus Jack points at the sky
E
Sandman canes Tommy Dreamer

Then Thunderkiss '65 *by White Zombie kicks in. Man, that tune rocks. And we get a whole bunch of longer clips, showing some of the most insane action you've ever seen. We get Luna screaming, Terry Funk brandishing his branding iron, The Gangstas running their mouths, The Public Enemy dancing in the ring with the whole audience waving their arms as one, a Scorpio tumbleweed (twisting somersault legdrop), Terry Funk hanging Rocco Rock from the balcony by a rope tied round his ankles, a dog-collared Rocco Rock moonsaulting Pitbull 2 through a table, the Pitbulls superbombing a jobber, THAT Tommy Dreamer chairshot on Raven, Bill Alfonso screaming into a mic, Scorpio dropping the bomb (moonsault legdrop), Stevie Richards prancing with a tag belt, Beulah showing some leg, Raven DDTing Tommy Dreamer on the floor, Public Enemy getting buried under chairs as Terry Funk and Cactus Jack call for more, and finally, we get world champion The Sandman posing with Woman, a cigarette, his cane and the belt. Then up flash the letters "ECW" and the words "Join The Revolution!" as Joey Styles cries "This is EXTREME!"*

You see how that works? You're a first-time viewer, remember. In the first 5 minutes of this TV show, you've heard two of your favourite songs, seen two mutant, steroid-ridden rhinos nearly kill two blokes who look the guy from your school who smoked Camels and always drank malt whisky when you were on cheap cider, and the guy at school who was in the chess club and was always listening to Napalm Death on his Walkman. Then you've seen a bunch of guys you'd kinda liked a few years ago, but you've gone off that wrestling a bit, because it's all crappy Hogan shit in WCW and all Mantaur and Skip and Zip and the Godwinns in the WWF. Above all, you've seen crazy moves, blood, guys who look different, crazy moves, blood and all kinds of stuff you just don't get in the big leagues. If you're a wrestling fan, you're so totally hooked already. If you're just a channel-surfer who happens to be into rock music or extreme sports, the show has probably got your attention. If you're just a channel-surfer who stopped on this for no other reason than that everything else looked shit, you're probably at least thinking "what the fuck is this?" That's the genius of Heyman's music videos, especially when he opens the show with them. Before he tells you it's a wrestling show, he's got you thinking you're watching MTV. He's not just setting some moves to music. He's integrating his stories into songs that 1) in many cases, are providing an interesting lyrical and cultural context for the feud to which they relate and 2) his audience digs.

Elsewhere on the show, Lance Wright would promote merchandise and live events in a frenzied sales pitch segment so shameless it could only have worked with its self-referential title of *Hype Central*. The promotion was spoofing the shameless commercialism of other wrestling groups, while achieving exactly the same goals. (In many ways, the 'secret' of ECW was that its fans were perfectly happy with the wrestling industry's inherent bullshit, just as long as promoters had the honesty to acknowledge it as such.) And Heyman, assisted by Ron Buffone & Charlie Bruzzese, continued to produce highlight videos backed by contemporary songs, mixing clips with the tune's original video, most notably the Guns N' Roses track *November Rain* in the now traditional preview of the November to Remember show.

That event would feature the conclusion of the period's best series of matches in an ECW ring, Rey Misterio Jr vs Psicosis. The pair had been brought in to replace the gap left by Benoit, Malenko and Guerrero (Heyman even billed them as direct replacements when he addressed the crowd on the WCW departees' farewell show). The later claim that this was the breakthrough feud for the smaller, Mexican wrestlers in the US was misleading; both men had appeared on the WCW produced AAA show *When Worlds Collide* and had appeared in front of large crowds in California and Chicago. Indeed, Eric Bischoff signed Misterio after seeing him at the independent World Wrestling Peace Festival show in Los Angeles in 1996. But the warm reaction to the pair (later joined in ECW by Konnan, La Parka and Juventud Guerrera) certainly showed the style could overcome initial prejudice in an area of the country hardly known for its Hispanic culture or a tolerance for undersized wrestlers.

The show also featured two events which would eventually lead to the promotion's biggest match. Following Sabu's departure, the Tazmaniac had been repackaged as the 'shooter' (legitimate amateur wrestler) Taz, but had suffered a serious neck injury thanks to a miscommunication in a tag match with Malenko and Scorpio in which he was unprepared for a spiked piledriver. Turning his legitimate bitterness at the lack of fan sympathy during his absence into a credible on-screen storyline, he turned against Tod Gordon while acting as a special referee, handing an unpopular victory to Bill Alfonso.

One of the storyline triggers for the turn (and no doubt a legitimate source of off-screen annoyance for Taz) came earlier in the show when Heyman announced that, to make up for the fire incident, he had a special surprise. It was the return of Sabu, for whom the timing couldn't have been better, having failed to make headway in New Japan (earning few discipline points for throwing down the company's junior-heavyweight title, claiming to be a heavyweight or nothing) and on the verge of being fired from a brief WCW stint, though he only received confirmation through the company's premium-rate hotline! Said Heyman to the *Pro Wrestling Torch* of the return "I have no problem humbling myself for the good of the company. This was right for business. The timing was perfect for marketing because everyone knows we owed them one."

But to Taz (both in character and reality), this amounted to forgiving a man who had abandoned both he as an in-ring partner, and the promotion as an employee. Taz vs Sabu would be the most heated match the company had to offer.

And they wouldn't even touch one another for a full year.

12: 1996

"If you take a WCW guy into your promotion, he's not going to draw because you don't have the total package. They are the greatest star in the world as long as they stay there." (Dennis Coraluzzo, RF Video interview)

It's sometimes said that Paul Heyman's greatest skill lay in hiding the weaknesses of performers and promoting their strong points to convince fans they were among the world's best wrestlers. But in some cases that manipulation even extended to other wrestling promoters. With hindsight, the idea that WWF and WCW engaged in a battle to secure the services of Public Enemy is laughable, but at the time both groups bought into the image rather than the reality. The first ECW Arena show of 1996 saw a fond farewell to Rock and Grunge as they became the first truly home-grown stars to depart for the big two. Though having wrestled a dark match tryout at the Survivor Series against the Smoking Gunns, they elected to take a job with WCW, set up in part by the warm relationship between Heyman and Kevin Sullivan. It was a running joke at the time that Sullivan also helped himself to ECW booking ideas, with wife Nancy, otherwise known as Woman, cited as the messenger; she too departed for WCW shortly after the New Year. This didn't stop the 'coincidences': for example, a May ECW TV show with satellite break-ins and audible production cues was remarkably similar to an incident where nWo wrestlers took over a production truck on *Nitro* later in the year. But while WCW programming was open to ideas from Philadelphia, it was still a land of generic music, 'safe' interviews, and undercard matches largely free of bleeding or weapons. It really should have come as no surprise that Public Enemy were quickly established as an non-threatening lower card act, a role they maintained in a later WWF run.

(The WWF appeared equally influenced by the combination of the Monday Night War and the ECW product. In the space of a month in late 1995 Bret Hart went through a table, Diesel became a character who was not a clear face or heel and gave reality based promos, Sid powerbombed Marty Jannetty on the arena floor, Shawn Michaels pulled off a particularly convincing 'collapse' on live TV, Bret was heavily bloodied on pay-per-view, and Goldust's character was revamped with heavy homosexual overtones.)

As was becoming a familiar pattern, ECW made sure to overcome the loss. The night of Public Enemy's departure saw the the debut of Rob Van Dam and the return of Shane Douglas (whose time in the WWF saw the backstage antics of Shawn Michaels and cronies collide with his own overly-passionate attitude to business to produce a less-than-memorable run). Heyman also took notable steps to protect the company's championships, with Raven (who took the ECW title from Sandman in late January), TV champ Scorpio and tag champs the Eliminators all putting across the message that the title belts were their most prized possessions.

The company also continued its slow but steady expansion, rising from 52 shows in 1995 to 67 in 1996. ECW ran several venues for regular monthly shows, with the Eliminators doing much of the local organisation in their native Massachusetts (a task that would eventually be taken on in Western Pennsylvania by Douglas, and nationally by Mark 'Buh Buh Ray Dudley' Lamonica and Lou 'Sign Guy' D'Angeli). And the promotion even debuted in Japan, with several wrestlers appearing as part of two IWA shows.

But the increased schedule wasn't without logistical problems. There were repeated complaints about shows starting late, tickets not being delivered on time, seats being sold twice, and 'reserved' seating being rendered useless when there was no form of numbered seating plan at the venue. New York events were particularly close to getting out of control, attracting fans who seemed more interested in the 'blood and guts' stereotype than traditional in-ring matches; one show in Queens almost had to be closed down because rowdy fans were throwing items at the ring. Elsewhere the Bruise Brothers earned a legitimate three-week suspension for throwing a chair into the crowd. Eliminator Perry Saturn took a more subtle approach, walking past a row of fans each holding up a chair in the hope a wrestler would use it, and 'accidentally' forearm-smashing the chairs into the fans' faces.

The television network continued to expand, with the show

carried by many local stations from the Prime Network early on Sunday mornings; though there were now clearances across the country, coverage was still a patchy, station-by-station set up and many major cities were not covered. Prime also took over Sportschannel Philadelphia (ECW's original TV home); new head Lorene Ong, a previous opponent of ECW's content, quickly axed the earlier of the promotion's two evening showings. Later in the year, Fox bought out the Prime Network, with the show being replaced in several markets by Fox's own sports coverage. Not all the problems were outside ECW's control: having picked up the show again after dropping it over the Mikey Whipwreck caning controversy, Florida's Sunshine Network axed the broadcast for a second time after the inclusion of a 'lesbian' kiss between rival valets Beulah McGillicutty and Kimona Wanaleia.

But controversy was still at the heart of ECW's promotional strategy, with a classic case being when a WCW wrestler threatened to urinate in the ECW Arena ring.

With his former high-flying style limited by injuries (and comparison to a new generation of cruiserweight wrestlers), Brian Pillman had begun a bizarre series of attempts to convince the wrestling world, on both sides of the curtain, that he was losing his mind. From supposedly real brawls with other wrestlers, to walking out in the middle of a PPV match with Kevin Sullivan (referring to him as the "bookerman"), he was soon spending as much time trying to fool colleagues and industry 'insiders' as he was the viewing public. By early February, he was publicly "suspended" as part of the insider-oriented storyline. So it was perhaps appropriate that he chose to debut in the ECW Arena on the CyberSlam show held on the weekend of a convention for internet fans. But even there the blurring of story and reality continued: after verbally attacking Eric Bischoff, he turned against the "smart mark" ECW fans and threatened to "whip out his Johnson and piss in the ring" prompting Heyman, Gordon and Douglas to storm the ring to give the impression he had broken from the script. Meanwhile the fans amused themselves with a bizarre chant of "Let him piss!" while Sign Guy's written message read "Don't work me, Pillman".

On this and future appearances, Pillman played the role of troublemaker both in front of the crowd and backstage, though he perhaps took things too far when he referred to the rap group Niggaz With Attitude during a ringside interview about the Gangstas; a backstage New Jack took it as a racial slur and had to be restrained from a legitimate fight when Pillman returned to the dressing room. Yet for all the controversy, it's unlikely Pillman's work ever directly drew much money for ECW: any plans for him to wrestle Douglas were put on hold when Pillman suffered a broken ankle in a car crash. Indeed, he was the only person to significantly profit on the deal, fooling WCW into legitimately releasing him from his contract to give the angle added credibility, then using his new-found freedom to sign for the WWF as one of the first men to ever received a guaranteed contract from Vince McMahon.

The WWF itself was the subject of another attempt to run credible angles or fool the hardcore fans (depending on your interpretation) in September. Heyman, Sandman and Tommy Dreamer acquired ringside tickets to an In Your House pay-per-view in Philadelphia, entered with the fans, and began mocking both wrestlers during a match pitting Savio Vega against Justin Hawk Bradshaw (ironically enough, JBL in a previous gimmick). Eventually Sandman sprayed beer at the pair, and all three 'invaders' were escorted from the building while the announcers made references to a local group based in a bingo hall. The following evening on *RAW*, Taz came to ringside and jumped the guard rail, holding up a "Sabu fears Taz" sign on live television; Bill Alfonso did not make it too far past the rails, having being tackled by an unsuspecting security guard.

Plans for the incidents were kept secret from all but those directly involved, and ECW even offered a cash reward to any fans who captured the incidents on camera (giving a cover story when they later showed what was clearly WWF footage on the ECW TV show). Meanwhile, in an AOL chat, McMahon claimed "The only deal between ECW and WWF is that ECW, if they have not already, will be hearing from our attorneys as a result of their intrusion on our pay-per-view and live *RAW*. As I recognise, this is America and ECW has just as much right to be in business as us. I would appreciate it if they did not interrupt our activities to gain notoriety."

And on an episode of WWF's call-in show *Livewire*, a man

calling himself Bruce from Connecticut (named after WWF official Bruce Prichard) but sounding remarkably like Paul Heyman, phoned in to chat to the WWF boss.

"Mr McMahon, I happen to agree with you that the E in ECW should have the word ego involved because isn't it your ego sir, that the WWF continues to steal concepts, ideas and talent from ECW without giving them the proper credit? Isn't it true Mr McMahon that it's your ego, that you're the one who wants to take the credit for the hardcore style of ECW... Shut up! You're interrupting while I'm talking. You think the nWo is extreme. You think Eric Bischoff's hairstyle is extreme. Why don't you invite your viewers to check out ECW? What the hell do you have to be afraid of? Why don't you shut the 'f' up?"

It was, of course, a prearranged deal intended to help promote ECW while giving WWF something to attract viewer interest to counter the overwhelming success of WCW's nWo angle. Tod Gordon later said he felt working with WWF on the angle was a betrayal of ECW's core values, but by this point such decisions were out of his hands. And Heyman's relationship with the WWF was certainly warmer than was apparent on screen; he and McMahon met cordially at the China Club, an old Heyman haunt, when the WWF was scouting venues for its new New York *Shotgun Saturday Night* show, while Gordon later claimed Heyman was on such good terms with Prichard that he would know within ten minutes if an ECW wrestler ever visited the WWF offices looking for work.

Back in ECW rings, the intricate booking continued as numerous storylines weaved together. Perhaps the ultimate example was the opening segment of the 13 February TV show. It began with Joey Styles attempting to introduce the show but being interrupted by Taz and Alfonso. Their gloating at having taken out 911 prompted his partner Rey Misterio Jr to come to the ring, state that he was not afraid of Taz, and begin a brawl, ending with Taz suplexing him into immobility. JT Smith and Hack Myers came to Misterio's aid, but Smith made mafia references before laying the boots to him. This prompted Myers to begin brawling with him amid the traditional "Shah!/Shit!" chants. As the pair brawled to the back, Styles attempted a second take of the introduction but was interrupted by the WCW-bound Woman, who ignored "You sold out!" chants, advised viewers to look out for her on Monday nights on TV, and suggested Styles might like to accompany her. This prompted the entrance of the Sandman (with music), but Woman challenged he or any other person to remove her. Too Cold Scorpio came to the ring and teased joining her, but instead carried her out of the building and dumped her in a limo, telling the driver "don't stop until Atlanta!". Back in the ring, Stevie Richards and the Blue Meanie were offering Sandman a final opportunity to back out of a match with Raven later in the night. When he rejected the offer, Richards threatened to superkick him, but instead had the Meanie make an elaborate but graceless attempt at the same move; Sandman caned him into oblivion and left. As Richards worried about the trouble he would be in, Raven and Kimona came to the ring, with Raven slapping Richards for failing to make sure the recently impregnated Beulah McGillicutty took her contraceptive pill. Stevie responded by saying he had a surprise that would make national news and began searching through Meanie's pockets (revealing all manner of unpleasant objects) before finding a legal document. Apparently made out in the name of "Dancing Stevie Richards, The Original King of Swing, Esquire", it was a sexual harassment lawsuit against Missy Hyatt, who had kissed him at the previous show in the building. As Richards made reference to a lawyer from Scarsdale, New York (prompting knowing glances from everyone who recognised the Richard Heyman reference), Hyatt came to the ring. She rejected an offer to join Raven, leading to Sandman returning and caning Raven until he left the ring. Hyatt then asked if Styles was 18 ("I was when this thing started!"), then told Sandman she would replace Woman as his valet, the pair celebrating with a cigarette and a beer as the show cut to commercial. In just 20 minutes, the sequence had either featured or referenced fourteen different characters.

In more conventional wrestling action, the most acclaimed in-ring series of the ECW year pitted Sabu against Van Dam. The pair's first meeting ended in an unpopular disqualification, provoking the unorthodox sight of booker Heyman going on the record in the *Pro Wrestling Torch* to say "I'm extremely pissed for not doing what was right. There should have been a decisive conclusion, a winner and a loser", comparing his own failing with a similarly criticised finish in the Bret Hart vs Undertaker main event of the WWF's previous pay-per-view. The follow up match, three months later, was billed as "must be a winner", with Sabu taking the nod after a series of innovative uses of ringside furniture. Following the match, Van Dam refused to shake Sabu's hand, earning him a round of boos (and no doubt planting a seed in the mind of Gabe Sapolsky). This led to a rematch on the next show where the loser had to proclaim his respect for the winner. To the crowd's shock, Sabu suffered a rare clean pinfall loss and lived up to the stipulation before offering a handshake, which Van Dam rejected with the simple-but-effective comment "I don't respect you; you're a piece of shit" before leaving the ring with Bill Alfonso.

Proof of the interest in the next bout in the series came when it took place past midnight, after an hour-long delay to fix a broken ring (which followed a 20 minute delay earlier in the show to repair a microphone). Virtually all of the crowd remained for the match despite offers of a refund, and they were rewarded (or pacified) with an impromptu striptease by Kimona on the main stage. The match itself could have fallen apart when the ring broke again after a few minutes, but the pair held the crowd's attention, with Sabu scoring the pin and Van Dam leaving on a stretcher. The only logical finish to the feud came with a stretcher match, in which Van Dam was again carried from the ring as the loser. Taken as a whole, the feud showed that there is more to character development than wins and losses: Van Dam only won one match, and was beaten cleanly three times, yet he ended the series firmly established as a top level star.

The pair later teamed up and began a series of matches with Dan Kroffat and Doug Furnas, who came into the group as part of a relationship with All Japan that also saw the ECW debuts of Johnny Smith and Steve Williams (who teamed up with the returning Terry Gordy). By the end of the year, Sabu and Van Dam were feuding with the Eliminators in a series of matches that were arguably a turning point in the development of the 'modern indy' style. For better or worse, these were among the first high-profile bouts where (to the target audience) the spectacular series of moves more than outweighed such criticisms as a lack of logical build to the bout, or blatantly obvious cooperation between opponents in setting up moves. While there had been criticism of the style of ECW matches before, this was perhaps the first time that such a clear philosophical chasm opened between those who advocated credibility and logic, and those for whom a hit-and-miss but always jaw-dropping spectacle outweighed all other concerns.

Elsewhere in the tag division, the Gangstas' arena-wide brawling eventually led to them becoming strong favourites among the crowd, with music again playing a central role. In place of the usual formalities, their matches consistently began with a fight across the building accompanied by *Natural Born Killaz* played in its entirety, producing a live spectacle akin to a music video come to life. There can be fewer more surreal sights in wrestling history than that of a thousand plus largely caucasian fans celebrating the Gangstas tag title win by erupting in joy and crossing their arms in a gesture that had its roots in black militant Malcolm X.

In a more traditional style, the TV title scene revolved around a series of matches with Chris Jericho, Scorpio, Douglas and Pitbull 2; all four men held the belt at some point in the build-up to a classic 39 minute elimination match won by Douglas when Francine turned against the Pitbulls. The feud gained an unintended boost when a Douglas DDT after the match left Pitbull 1 with a broken neck (though his huge build meant it was a couple of days before he realised how serious the injury was and saw a doctor); both men, to this day, dispute who was truly responsible for the mishap. On television there was no dispute: the heel Douglas engaged in a series of defences against Pitbull 2 where the supposedly 'smart' fans found it remarkably easy to suspend their disbelief. Pitbull 1 began appearing at ringside in a surgical halo; although the need for the device was real, it seems likely he exaggerated the effects of the injury by letting one arm hang loose and numb. Fans who 'knew' the injury was legitimate were outraged when Douglas went on to grab him by the halo and throw him to the ground; Douglas described the response as "white heat", with a moment of shocked silence among the crowd before mayhem ensued. Douglas's interviews not only made fun of his rivals, but mocked the fans for proclaiming to be hardcore and unshockable, yet reacting in disgust to his actions.

The response to Douglas was certainly in stark contrast to that for the antics of Tommy Dreamer and Brian Lee. Brought in by Raven to deal with Dreamer, Lee began a series of chokeslams from increasingly dangerous places. One show saw Dreamer crash from a balcony through several tables, while another saw him thrown from atop a cage. At one point fans were almost beginning to expect a truly life-threatening drop from atop the Arena itself. Like all good feuds, it ended with the babyface Dreamer gaining revenge in a stipulation match, this being a 'High Incident' bout, Lee's loss coming in the form of being thrown from a scaffold through a pile of tables stacked throughout the ring. (Dreamer retired from full-time competition, due in part to the continuing effects of a career of injuries, shortly before his 33rd birthday.)

With Dreamer occupied, Raven's main focus turned to Sandman, with a series of controversial angles in which he 'stole' Sandman's wife Lori and his young son Tyler (whose stoic expression and deadpan delivery almost outshone that of Raven). The bizarre disparity between wrestling storyline and reality came into play when Raven's real life drug problems became so serious that he took time off to address them. Jim Fullington drove his friend Scott Levy to rehab, then went to the Arena the same night and, as Sandman, pinned stand-in Stevie Richards to capture rival Raven's ECW title thanks to a pre-match stipulation. When Raven returned to the company, he regained the title in a barbed wire match (a stipulation Heyman insisted on as a condition for the title change), but not before a controversial incident in which Raven and company tied Sandman to a wooden crucifix (ironically built by Sandman himself, whose day job was in construction) and placed a barbed wire 'crown' on his head. Unfortunately this went down badly with a guest for the night, freshly crowned Olympic champion Kurt Angle. While coincidental, it didn't help that this Christianity-based angle was carried out by one Jewish man (Raven) in a company run by two others (Heyman and Gordon). With hindsight, most involved consider the angle's failings were not as serious a mistake as when Raven was then told to go to the ring, break character, and apologise, which he did with a lack of sincerity outstanding even by professional wrestling standards.

There was some light relief in the Raven storylines, in the form of Richards and the Meanie. The pair would regularly dress up and spoof wrestling gimmicks of the past, from Diesel (Big Daddy Fool) and Shawn Michaels (Heartburn Kid), to the Blue Bloods (Sir Meanie of Eating, rather than Eaton), to the Fabulous Ones, to Bluedust, to Baron Von Stevie, to Public Enemy. (Within a couple of years, such spoofs were commonplace on Monday Nights, be it WWF's Degeneration X and Nation of Domination spoofing one another, or Kevin Nash and friends mocking the Four Horsemen). In one case Meanie and Richards were joined by Nova and Don E Allen to become the rock band Knights In Stevie's Service (KISS). And most famously, Big Stevie Cool, Da Blue Guy and Hollywood Nova formed the Blue World Order, a gimmick so successful it stuck for more than six months and at one point accounted for half the promotion's merchandise sales.

Laughter was not a strong point for Taz, however. Behind the scenes he and Perry Saturn ran the company's 'House of Hardcore' training school, with Taz's cousin Chris Chetti and Roadkill among the early graduates of the no-frills, dojo style facility. Trainees would then appear on-screen as part of 'Team Taz', a silent entourage aimed at enforcing his character of a hard-hitting shootfighter for whom every opponent was a chokeout away from becoming "just another victim". He even stood straight up from a 911 chokeslam and choked him out. (911 then got up quickly himself against booking orders, causing his firing and some hasty editing of the tape.) The most infamous Taz victory came when, after defeating legitimate mixed martial artist Jason Helton, he took on Ultimate Fighting Championship finalist Paul Varalens, who had more than a foot's advantage in height. It's a measure of how successfully Taz was pushed that many fans assumed (rightly or wrongly) that he could have beaten Varalens in a truly legitimate contest. In the instance Varalens was persuaded to take the loss (allegedly on an undelivered promise of sexual relations with Missy Hyatt) but insisted on outside interference; this came courtesy of a dropkick to the head by Perry Saturn delivered with such force that Taz was left to suplex the deadweight of the mammoth fighter.

The year-long build, in which Taz repeatedly made the unanswered claim that Sabu was afraid to face him, climaxed at November to Remember, the first ECW Arena show to sell out before the day of the event. Too Cold Scorpio, who would debut for the WWF the following night, issued a series of challenges for any wrestler to force him out of the company. Devon Storm, JT Smith and Hack Myers lost quick matches to him, being forced themselves to leave the company for 15, 30 and 60 days respectively; all three stood by the stipulations. Louie Spicolli then beat Scorpio, forcing him out of ECW for a year, but he refused to leave the building. However, Taz cleared him from the ring and grabbed the microphone.

As he spoke in the ring, the arena lights went out. When they came back on, Sabu was standing in the ring, and the pair locked up for the first time in two and a half years, causing an overwhelming ovation. Seconds later the lights went back out again, and both men had departed when they came back on. The fans had been given a brief taster, but everyone knew that the match itself was being saved for the company's expected early 1997 pay-per-view debut.

But a week later that wasn't so certain.

13: Revere

"I wish the kid would have fucking died, because he makes what I do look bad." (Perry Saturn, CyberSlam Q&A session, February 1997)

Jerome Young never claimed to be the model employee.

As New Jack, he had already been involved in several brushes with authority during his ECW spell (in addition to the Pillman incident). In October 1995 he was involved in a series of stiff exchanges in the ring after Dances With Dudley complained he was working too recklessly and had caused a broken nose. New Jack then attacked him backstage with a nightstick, with other wrestlers breaking up the incident before it developed further. The Gangstas were officially fired over the incident, but in practice it was more of a suspension as they returned to action at the end of December.

The following February, New Jack missed an Arena show having been incarcerated. According to an interview he gave on the next show "A guy owed me money and he didn't pay me back, so I kicked his ass and locked him in the trunk of my car. I got arrested because I left the guy in there too long and the cops had to let him out." (Bizarrely this was the moment the ECW regulars accepted the Gangstas as full-fledged babyfaces.) And at the 30 March Arena show, a squash match against Blue Meanie and Chad Austin appeared to go beyond the expected norm of simulated combat, with New Jack brutalising Austin with several stiff chair shots to the knees and legs. New Jack boasted that he broke Austin's leg, though Austin later said the beating was not as vicious as many believed.

But these incidents would all be overshadowed by the events of 23 November 1996.

A 17-year-old named Eric Kulas, who weighed around 400 pounds, talked his way backstage at an ECW show in Revere, Massachusetts. He had wrestled something between 10 and 15 matches on small shows in the New England area, mainly comedy matches where he worked as 'Ralph Kramden' (the name of a bus-driving Jackie Gleason character in *The Honeymooners*) against two midgets, who were with him in Revere. He hoped to perform with the midgets on the ECW show.

Axl Rotten had not appeared as planned and Paul Heyman, facing a reshuffle of the card, discussed the possibility of Kulas taking his place to team with D Von Dudley against the Gangstas. According to Heyman, Kulas claimed to be 19 and to have been trained by Wladek 'Killer' Kowalski. (There appear to have been no steps taken to confirm the latter claim, though legitimate Kowalski trainee Perry Saturn was on the show.) Kulas agreed to work the match, using the name 'Mass Transit' (to fit in with his ring gear of a bus driver uniform), and annoyed several people backstage by suggesting offensive moves he could deliver, apparently having wildly misunderstood his role for the night.

What happened next has been widely misreported based on eyewitness accounts. The building had no raised seating and a particularly low roof, making visibility very poor for much of the audience. However, what really happened was captured on camcorder for RF Video's fancam series.

The videotape starts with D Von and Kulas in the ring, with Kulas telling the crowd "Fuck you!" and gesturing that they should kiss his behind; the crowd responded with chants of "You fat fuck!". New Jack and Mustafa hit the ring, with New Jack carrying a garbage can full of miscellaneous objects, which he emptied on the canvas. As Mustafa floored Kulas and began kicking him, the camera followed New Jack and D Von into the crowd. New Jack returned alone and entered the ring with a two-on-one advantage on Kulas.

New Jack twice hit the floored Kulas in the back with a crutch, then smashed him hard in the head with the remnants of a guitar and then a toaster. At this point D Von had returned to ringside, but was knocked from the ring apron to the floor. A voice, later identified as Kulas' father Steve, is audible on the tape, shouting "Take it easy on him!" and "He's just a kid!"

New Jack then took out what was reported to be an Xacto knife (the US equivalent of a Stanley knife), but appears on the tape to match New Jack's description of a surgical scalpel attached to a makeshift wooden handle. He then held the scalpel to Kulas' forehead and rocked the handle back and forth nine times (the blade cutting or sawing into the skin), the final time being notably more forceful than the others and prompting a loud scream from Kulas. Despite later reports, he did not make any stabbing motion, nor drag the handle to produce a slicing motion, and Kulas' head remained still throughout the event. At no point during the match did Kulas appear to make efforts to actively defend himself.

Kulas then turned over to his hands and knees, with a thick torrent of blood immediately pouring to the floor. As Kulas Sr shouted "That's enough!", New Jack hit Kulas with an unclear object that may have been the handle of a 'cat o'nine tails', prompting Kulas Sr to add "Get him the fuck out of here, he's 17, ring the fucking bell!" As the crowd began a chant of "ECW", New Jack hit Kulas in the head with the garbage can, then punched D Von in the head as he attempted to climb into the ring. Mustafa picked up Kulas for a sloppy bodyslam; although he was aware enough to attempt to assist in the move, Kulas lost his grip, causing Mustafa to drop him earlier than is usual in the move. New Jack then came off the top turnbuckle with a chair to the head and covered Kulas for a visual three count (there is no sight of a referee at any point during the film sequence).

Kulas was now lying on his back, with a close-up zoom shot showing that blood was spraying upwards from his forehead, resembling a fountain. The 'Damage Control' medics came to the ring and began working on him, using first a cloth and then a towel to stem the blood flow. New Jack then addressed the crowd; much of what he said was inaudible beyond a string of obscenities, but it concluded "I hope this fat piece of shit don't leave the fucking building, because I don't give a fuck". (Claims that New Jack more specifically said he hoped Kulas died are not borne out by the footage.) New Jack and Mustafa then left the ring to their music. Medics were attaching a fluid drip to Kulas as the filming ended, not resuming until the following match started. (The battery in the camcorder had run out and needed changing. Had it run out a few minutes earlier, the incident might never have gained such notoriety or had such consequences.)

According to reports, an ambulance was then called, while medics began using t-shirts to soak up the blood, having ran out of towels. It was estimated that it took ten minutes to finally staunch the bleeding. Once Kulas was taken from the ring, members of the ring crew mopped up the mat before the next match. Kulas received around 50 stitches at hospital. Several wrestlers reported that, while being stretchered from the ring, Kulas had asked if he had performed well and would be welcome back. Betsy Sherman of the *Improper Bostonian* magazine, who audio-taped an interview with Heyman on the night, quoted him as saying "He's a good kid" and "He got initiated".

Speaking in the *Pro Wrestling Torch* shortly after the incident, Heyman claimed New Jack had used a razor blade, and that the severity of the gash was caused by Kulas jerking his head. (This is clearly disproven by the videotape.) He added that he had offered to pay all medical bills, and that in future he would insist all potential ECW wrestlers went to the company's training centre and proved their competence before being booked on a live event. Heyman then advised New Jack not to speak about the event because of potential legal issues. He was pulled from all shows in Massachusetts, missing six shows in Revere before performing a run-in in October 1997 and then returning to the ring at the December 1997 show.

RF Video released the tape of the show on home video (one account says they sold between 30 and 40 copies) but withdrew it on ECW orders a week after the incident. This proved ineffective, as the tape was widely copied and circulated among hardcore wrestling fans. (After the closure of ECW, RF Video began selling the tape again.) Steve Kulas obtained a copy of the tape from RF Video, apparently giving the impression he wanted it as a souvenir, though this may have been a cover story on his part to avoid tipping off that he was looking for evidence. The tape later appeared on several local television news programmes, though the goriest parts were not broadcastable.

Though Steve Kulas initially claimed he was not interested in taking legal action, he later hired a lawyer to press criminal charges. At first a judge ruled against indicting New Jack on the grounds that it would be too difficult to distinguish between performance and reality in pro wrestling. However, a second judge heard evidence on 21 July 1997 from New Jack and Kulas. New Jack said Kulas had seen and approved all the weapons to be used in the match, and requested that New Jack cut him open; Kulas denied saying this. The judge ruled that, while he was unfamiliar with how wrestling operated, the videotape was enough to warrant further legal scrutiny, calling both men, plus Heyman and Tommy Dreamer to a 5 August hearing. This hearing produced no outcome as the judge delayed a decision, suggesting the case may be more appropriate for the civil courts. By this point the case had been taken over from the Kulas' lawyer by a District Attorney (the US equivalent of the Crown Prosecution Service). A further hearing concluded there was enough evidence to move to a trial, which was originally set for April 1999, but delayed until 26 May after an attorney was double-booked (a problem apparently not unique to pro wrestling).

New Jack claims to have been offered, and rejected, a plea-bargain under which he would receive five years imprisonment (the maximum sentence for the charges was 17 years). He was charged with aggravated assault and assault with a deadly weapon.

Kulas' testimony in the trial was extremely ill-advised as he claimed he was ambushed in the match and had no expectation of being cut. This was contradicted by New Jack, Heyman, D Von and Dreamer, who all testified that he was aware he would be facing the Gangstas and had asked to be cut open; one of the midget wrestlers also disputed Kulas' story. Dreamer said he was with Kulas throughout most of the evening, and that following the match Kulas asked if he had proven himself and earned a job. The court heard that Kulas had taken part in a match with similar weapon use on an independent show a few weeks before the Revere incident. The jury saw the video tape of the incident, but the close-up shot of the spurting blood and New Jack's comments on the microphone were both removed from the tape after the judge ruled they were too prejudicial and not relevant to the factual decision as to whether New Jack committed assault.

The jury began deliberations late on a Wednesday and returned early on the Thursday to deliver a verdict of not guilty on both counts.

New Jack's attorney James Merberg said "This was absolutely not a staged assault on an innocent young man, but rather a choreographed, planned match." The prosecuting District Attorney

Michael Murphy said the jury may have been confused by the nature of professional wrestling. "I think they believed that the alleged victim was a willing participant in the event and that maybe the defendant made a mistake or that it was an accident that he hurt him so bad, but that it was part of the routine."

The Kulas family then filed civil suits against New Jack, Heyman, ECW (HHG Corp), the building owners and others. Most of these suits were dismissed by courts and none had come to trial when Kulas died on 12 May 2002 at the age of 22 of a condition related to his extreme obesity.

14: The Road to Pay-Per-View

"On Sunday Night April 13, we're gonna show the whole fucking world what we've got here because despite cancellations and despite the threat of lawsuits, because of your cards and your letters and your e-mails and the vociferousness of this audience, because you chant ECW, because you always give us a second chance, this show will be carried live on pay-per-view!" (Paul Heyman, ECW Arena, 1 February 1997)

For a company that lived day-to-day and almost prided itself on its 'on the fly' booking, ECW's move to get on pay-per-view was anything but an overnight step. Having previously said the company was not ready, Paul Heyman's first reported steps came in the summer of 95 when he considered an approach to the TVKO and Semaphore Groups (promoters of boxing and Ultimate Fighting Championship events respectively). By October that year, ECW was in talks with the William Morris entertainment agency to promote pay-per-view events on a tape delay of one or two days. Throughout 1996, it was clear such events were firm plans: Heyman tempted Shane Douglas back to ECW with promises of PPV exposure, while the company began securing the rights to use their existing entrance music on such broadcasts. The timescale slowly crept backwards, but by late in the year it seemed likely the event would take place in the spring of 1997, particularly after around 10 wrestlers signed six-month exclusive contracts. Viewers Choice turned down the opportunity to carry the event after seeing a demo tape which included footage of the Raven-Sandman storyline, notably a clip when Sandman threatened to cane his young son Tyler, but Request TV, the other major PPV distributor, was considering carrying the show and even suggesting a live broadcast.

Then came Revere.

What really happened in the month following the event is the increasingly familiar story of conflicting accounts and accusations. Assuming that all direct accounts of conversations by an involved party are accurate (which is a potentially naive but unavoidable approach), the chronology was as follows:

    * During the week of the Revere show, Heyman told the *Pro Wrestling Torch* that it was almost certain a PPV date would be finalised in the coming days. Request TV never publicly committed to carrying the show, but an unconfirmed account of 'an ECW source' suggests that at some point the company expected to sign an agreement on 28 December.

    * On 3 December (ten days after Revere), Heyman told the *Torch* "The tape [of the Revere

incident] has been seen by everybody who is in a decision-making position that regards anything in our future, including [the pay-per-view firms]. They were all notified Monday morning that we had an incident, that it most probably was going to cause bad publicity, and that we wanted to be the first ones to alert them to the situation, tell them our side of the story, and give them a tape so that three months down the road it's not like 'Oh My God! You told me it was bad, but I didn't know it was this bad.' 'Here it is guys, this is how bad it is, if you're going to tell me to fuck off, tell me now.'"

    * On 19 December, the *Torch* contacted Request TV and asked its president Hugh Panero if the pay-per-view date had been finalised. Panero said he was unsure, and that some issues still had to be worked out. Asked if these issues or the delay involved the content of the demo tape, or the tape ECW had sent of the Revere incident, Panero said he did not know but would find out.

    * On 20 December, Panero told the *Torch* that Request TV had finalised its decision that day, and would not be carrying the event. He cited two incidents (the fire problem in October 1995 and the Revere incident) as being things they could not look past. He added that nobody at Request knew of the Revere incident before the previous day (19 December), that nobody at the company had seen a tape, and that Request had called ECW that day (20 December) and they had described the incident in detail. He also said "It's a stretch of the imagination if [ECW] are saying they provided us with a tape to let us know of these incidents. We never received a tape."

* On 23 December, Heyman told the Torch that "Request TV was sent a tape, knew of the incident [and] was aware of the situation", adding that he had never spoken to Panero and that the tape was not sent to him personally. On the same day, Panero said the decision to not carry the event was "pretty much final".

* On 25 December, Dave Scherer (editor of the *Wrestling Lariat*) posted in an internet newsgroup that a source at Request TV had told him the Revere incident was "brought to our attention by a wrestling newsletter writer from Minnesota. The writer explained the incidents in great depth, and even told us how to get tapes when we did not know what he was referring to." (The *Torch* is based in Minnesota.)

* On 26 December, *Torch* columnist Bruce Mitchell discussed the Request TV situation in his weekly update on the *Wrestling Observer* hotline. Bob Ryder (whose known involvement with ECW at that point involved arranging interviews with wrestlers and providing live play-by play of Arena shows, both for the Prodigy On-Line service) reported the content of the hotline as follows. "Mitchell spends the better part of 15 minutes preaching about the sins of ECW and taking credit for the fact that he and [*Torch*] editor Wade Keller had contacted Request officials to make them aware of the Mass Transit situation. Mitchell also implies he and Keller made the tape available to Request officials and says 'ECW should have burned the tape when they had the chance'. Observer Hotline messages normally remain active for 24 hours, but the Mitchell message was altered and all reference to involvement by Mitchell or Keller had been removed by 8am Central this morning. The message still concerned the cancellation of the ECW PPV, and still contained much of the same information as the original update, but all reference to involvement on the part of Mitchell and Keller had been removed." Mitchell later denied making such comments on the hotline.

* On 26 and 27 December, ECW and Request TV held a

conference call to discuss the problems with ECW content and the steps needed to remain on PPV.

      * On 30 December, Panero told the *Torch* it was still possible the event could air on Request TV. "We have not ruled out carrying them. But we need to know they are self-regulating." He said he had received about 40 e-mails from ECW fans complaining about the decision not to carry the event. "I find this whole thing almost childish," he said. "The issue would dissipate if ECW would just address the issues rather than inciting their cult following over this." He also repeated his denial of Request receiving a tape of the Revere incident, either from ECW or a third party. "We have never received a tape of this incident from anybody. If people think ECW sent us a tape to let us know about the problem, that's not true."

      * On 31 December, Panero issued a press release saying "We were surprised that ECW never mentioned that these public relations problems existed, and contrary to the claims made by ECW, no tape of the incident was sent to anyone at Request TV." On the same day, Ryder issued an apology reading "In my reporting of the events that led to the decision by Request TV to cancel the ECW PPV, I stated that Wade Keller and Bruce Mitchell had provided a tape of the Mass Transit incident to officials of Request TV. That turns out not to be the case. Request officials do not have a copy of the tape. My comments on the matter were based on my interpretation of the Wrestling Observer Hotline Report filed by Bruce Mitchell at midnight on December 25/26... a report that was pulled only a few hours after it went active. I apologize for the error."

      Once all the fuss had died down, the important point was that ECW and Request worked out the problems (as well as the Revere incident, Request were initially uneasy about the event because they mistakenly believed it to be a legitimate contest in the style of the Ultimate Fighting Championship). On 23 January Panero publicly announced they would carry the event, to be titled Barely Legal, on 13 April. The show would be live but at a later timeslot than usual for wrestling (9pm rather than 7pm) for $19.95. ECW agreed to meet Request's concerns by having a doctor at ringside with the power to stop a match, having an ambulance on standby, insuring the wrestlers, having an accredited police officer present, and getting Request's approval for any weapons which would be used (in the words of Tod Gordon "they wanted nothing pointy"). In return, ECW would be allowed to use their own director (Ron Buffone) and have Styles as the lone announcer, the first solo performance in wrestling pay-per-view history. Heyman formally announced the deal at the 1 February Arena show with the quote that opens this chapter. Perhaps as a dry run for the pay-per-view, it wasn't until the penultimate bout on that night's nine-match show that any matches spilled into the crowd.

The question of a how a company with no national television successfully promotes a pay-per-view was answered sixteen days later when Jerry Lawler berated a fan holding an ECW sign at a live edition of *RAW*; later in the show Heyman called in and accepted Lawler's challenge to bring ECW to the following week's show at the Manhattan Center. That show, taking place while half the WWF roster was on tour in Germany, alternated between WWF and ECW matches. The Eliminators took out a 'ring attendant' before Richards (accompanied by the rest of the bWo) beat Little Guido, with Raven looking on. Taz beat Mikey Whipwreck in a match best remembered for Sabu diving from the giant letter R which made up the *RAW* entranceway set, but slipping and almost landing on his head. And Dreamer pinned D Von Dudley in a weapons-filled bout ending with Buh Buh and Sandman involved in a brawl. Though the crowd was overwhelmingly behind ECW, Lawler continued verbally attacking the promotion, drawing attention to Taz's lack of height. (To be fair, Taz, unused to the larger WWF rings, did bang his head against the top rope while throwing Whipwreck to the outside.) Heyman replied with "Coming from a guy that's 5'10" who was on top of a territory for 76 years, that's the most ridiculous thing I've ever heard."

The angle continued over the following two weeks with Heyman continuing to plug the pay-per-view, and he and Lawler engaging in a debate littered with insider references to Lawler's sons (who did not acknowledge their parenthood while wrestling) and his previous brushes with the law involving an unproven charge of statutory rape of a teenager. While entirely scripted, the debate was clearly intended to raise questions about whether either man had 'gone too far' on live television.

While officially the two promotions were simply working the angle for mutual benefit (publicity for ECW's pay-per-view, a newsmaking addition to *RAW*'s content), speculation began running rampant about their relationship. While suggestions that WWF helped fund the pay-per-view as an investment opportunity seem unlikely, the two companies **did** have a direct financial relationship, which was naturally kept quiet for fear of a backlash from loyal ECW followers. Speaking a couple of days before the first *RAW* angle, Heyman intimated to fans at a Q&A session that WWF had approached ECW to set up the angles the previous September ("Anytime somebody in this industry takes the time to call, I'd be a fool not to listen") and revealed that plans to extend the relationship (connected to WWF naming a house show tour "Holiday Hell", a name previously used by ECW) were discussed but dropped because he didn't like the direction.

What he didn't reveal at this point was that since at least the time of the original angles (and possibly as far back as late-1995), WWF had been paying ECW $1,000 a week. McMahon had apparently offered to put Heyman on the company payroll as compensation for taking ECW talent, with Heyman instead asking for the money to be paid as a fee to HHG Corp for talent development services.

On closer examination, this arrangement seems curious. The amount involved was nowhere close to making a serious difference in the big picture of ECW's finances, and would be unlikely to give McMahon significant power in threatening to withdraw it. McMahon's later claim that Heyman was working to steer departing talent towards joining the WWF rather than WCW appears shaky: until late 1999, WCW took a notable majority of those leaving ECW, particularly the more important characters, while several of those going to the WWF were former WCW wrestlers for whom a return to that promotion was never on the cards.

Given the personalities of the two men, the formal details of the arrangement were probably little more than nominal points that served the greater purpose of producing a better relationship between the pair. McMahon most likely saw an opportunity to pay what he saw as a cheap price to ensure an ally in his increasingly bitter war with WCW, while Heyman probably saw a way to keep on good terms with a potential predator while being able to justify to himself that he had not compromised his independence. A more cynical interpretation would be that, having burned his bridges with WCW, a healthy relationship with McMahon would be a wise insurance policy when running such a financially precarious operation as ECW.

Although many small independent cable systems carried the show thanks to calls from local customers, the absence of distribution by Viewers Choice meant Barely Legal would be available in somewhere between 12-14 million homes, compared to the 25-30 million for WWF and WCW shows. Heyman was quite open about the fact that the pay-per-view had no chance of making a profit, describing it as a chance to prove they could maintain their style while operating within the confines required by cable companies, with a successful show opening the doors to future events being more widely carried to the point that they could make money. He insisted the company was financially ready for the show: "If not one person buys the PPV, there's still an ECW on Monday April 14. There's nothing worth risking this whole thing for. If you told me to bet everything that is ECW and if the sun rises tomorrow you'll double it, I won't take that bet."

But while the finances were apparently secure, the pressure to perform was still causing unprecedented stress levels in the company. A couple of weeks before Barely Legal, two wrestlers brawling in the crowd on a show in Western Pennsylvania knocked over the merchandise table, causing a free-for-all as fans helped themselves. Shane Douglas, who promoted the show, blew his top and somehow wound up nose to nose with Tracey Smothers backstage after shouting about WWF spies. At another event Douglas got into a shoving match with Sandman. Steve Richards losing a match on an independent show became a major issue when other ECW wrestlers accused him of doing the wrong thing with his upcoming feature match to protect.

But come Sunday 13 April, wrestling's greatest motivational speaker would harness that stress and turn it into pure effort and enthusiasm.

15: Barely Legal

"It is 8:25pm. At 8:30, on whatever affiliates are picking us up, in 17 million homes, whether they've ordered the pay-per-view or not, our pre-game show starts. Three years ago we stood in that part of the dressing room. Eddie Gilbert left and Tod took a chance on a different concept. On a group of guys that nobody else wanted. On misfits who couldn't keep a job or didn't want one or shouldn't have had one to begin with, myself included.

"For three-and-a-half years we have survived and we have come together every three weeks in this building and we've come through the good times and the bad times. We've suffered injuries, we've suffered loss, we've suffered talent raids, we've suffered personal crises, we've suffered divisions in our dressing room. We suffered through the stress getting to us and the pressure about to crack us, but when push came to shove this dressing room stayed together.

"17 million homes that have pay-per-view capability will pay twenty dollars, hopefully, for the privilege of seeing you guys do what you have done for the last three and a half years. Thank Terry Funk for all that he has done for this company, for putting us on the map, for being unselfish, for taking the young guys and showing them a better way, Tonight we have a chance to say 'Yeah, you're right, we're too extreme, too wild, too out of control, we're too full of our own shit.' Or we have a chance to say 'Hey, fuck you, you're wrong. Fuck you, we're right', because we have all made it to the dance, and believe me, this is the dance.

"Tonight we have a chance to prove them right or prove them wrong. This is as big of an opportunity as we're gonna have, because if this works, if this is the show that in my heart I know this crew can put on, then we get a second one on August 17th and a third one in November and we go on from there. So we actually start to make some real [money] and we actually start to have a real life, and we actually start to pay our bills and not have to worry about next month's rent, or buy a home, or have a child, or have a family.

"This is what you have worked for. We have this opportunity

because I believe in this group. Not that my belief should mean goddamn anything to any of you. Your own belief in yourself is paramount. This is your show. I can't do anything more for you. It's yours to fail, or it's yours to succeed. My money's on you. I know this crew, I believe in this crew, so help me God, I love this fucking crew. Give these people the show of a fucking lifetime and we'll be back on pay-per-view August 17th. The ball is yours. Score, motherfuckers, score." (Paul Heyman, 13 April 1997)

Everything was ready. The banquet of honour for Terry Funk the previous evening had come off as the classy event it was meant to be. The new camera angles were set up. The new ring canvas was in place. The ECW Arena was, for perhaps the first time in years, spotlessly clean. The dark matches, Louie Spicolli beating Balls Mahoney and JT Smith making a surprise appearance to team with Chris Chetti over Tommy Rich and Little Guido, went to plan and finished on time. Countless hours of work had paid off with a pre-game show that had everything from House of Pain to The Eagles to accompany thirty minutes of relentless hype. The injured Mikey Whipwreck, of all people, was running the sound booth. Joey Styles was in the ring to introduce the show. Everything was ready.

And then somebody realised the ring microphone was broken ten seconds before airtime.

So it was that ECW's first exposure on pay-per-view was a lingering twenty seconds of Joey Styles looking bemused while off-screen voices from the production truck debated technical problems. But, aptly, the crowd saved the show, the scene of a thousand people rabidly chanting the company's initials more atmospheric than any video package or pyrotechnic display.

The show proper kicked off with the Eliminators regaining the tag titles from the Dudleys in a display that featured little traditional grappling, told no discernible story, was ridiculously convoluted... and was spectacular as hell. As a match, it was questionable. As a showcase for ECW as an alternative to mainstream wrestling, it was perfect.

It was a similar story in the following match as Rob Van Dam (replacing the injured Chris Candido) defeated Lance Storm.

While the match was designed to display Van Dam's fast-paced offence, it was Storm who passed into history, partly for the ugliest rat tail mullet ever seen in a televised match, and partly for a chairshot that, while showing an admirable attempt to avoid recklessly injuring an opponent, appeared so weak it might not have damaged a meringue. As fans greeted Van Dam's win with "You sold out" chants (based on rumours he was looking at a WCW deal, fuelled by him visiting friends backstage at a *Nitro* broadcast), he responded "I sold out to myself by putting my boots on and getting in the ring tonight, after obviously being chosen as a second-line wrestler to fill in for someone injured. Rob Van Dam is no second-line anything. I swallowed my pride for one reason: business. Because you see, Lance Storm, by beating you here, Rob Van Dam is now worth more money here, and Rob Van Dam is now worth more money elsewhere."

Where some promotions would be upset by outsiders stealing the show and outshining the resident performers, ECW had no such concerns. The Michinoku Pro six-man with Great Sasuke, Gran Hamada and Masato Yakushiji over Taka Michinoku, Terry Boy and Dick Togo proved both spectacular and fluid, the easy match of the night.

Following an interview where Steve Richards likened his career to a lonely teenager who never got a date (almost certainly resonating with many ECW fans), Shane Douglas defended the TV title against Pitbull 2. Sadly some of the steam of their heated feud seemed to have been lost, and the pressure of live television seemed to be a problem, with Pitbull quickly becoming winded and Douglas living up to his reputation of being able to be half of a great match-up, but struggling when it came to carrying an opponent. This being the longest match of the night proved a miscalculation and Douglas' win was easily overshadowed by a post-match angle. A masked man had been taunting Douglas for several months, and the distinctive walk and voice made it no secret that Rick Rude lay under the hood. But just as the mysterious figure came to ringside, one of Douglas' security staff (clad in riot gear) removed his helmet and revealed himself as Rude. At this exact moment, a stunned Douglas was removing the his tormentor's mask, revealing his Triple Threat stable partner Brian Lee, who formally introduced himself with a chokeslam.

Thanks to technical problems with a video shoot, Raven was then forced to deliver an interview live from the steps leading from the locker room to the main stage, with the entire roster keeping silent in the background.

Back in the ring, the story going back three and a half years came to its climax as Sabu and Taz finally squared off. By all rights their contrasting styles should have clashed in ugly fashion, but somehow it worked. Other than a miscue leaving Sabu running to the ring before his introduction and music, the match couldn't have gone better. It was certainly rough around the edges, but that only added to the grudge match feel, with the pair working their mutual unease into the match rather than failing to co-operate. After Taz took the win by chokeout, he shook Sabu's hand only for Van Dam to come to the ring and join Sabu in a beatdown, with Bill Alfonso announcing he was now Sabu's manager. Unlike many 'shock' double-turns, this one came with a logical explanation: according to Alfonso, he thought Taz might lose, bet heavily on Sabu as an insurance policy, and had now lost his money! (Though how he had a Sabu t-shirt under his regular formal shirt was not explained.) Meanwhile Van Dam furthered his storyline by informing any other promotion that was interested to contact him through Alfonso. "Fonzie knows my schedule, and I love to work Mondays!"

The good news was that the Sandman vs Richards vs Terry Funk number one contender match was fun, albeit it a particularly violent type of fun involving a ladder and barbed wire. The bad news was that it went so long that Funk's resulting title match with Raven started at the 2 hour 37 minute mark, a point at which most pay-per-view main events are approaching their closing moments. Fortunately Raven's self-confessed "dog and pony show" style of title match was easily adaptable, with the pair dropping the using formalities of building a lengthy bout and instead skipping straight to the bullet points: Funk's heavy bleeding caused a doctor to consider stopping the match; Raven knocked out the doctor (Mark Andrews, his real life roommate of the time); All Japan Women performer Reggie Bennett came out and powerbombed Funk; Big Dick Dudley appeared on the balcony where Tommy Dreamer was doing guest commentary and attempted to chokeslam him through a set of tables set up by mysterious bikers; Dreamer reversed the move and sent Dudley crashing; Raven floored the referee; Dreamer ran in and DDTed Raven for a false finish; Funk scored the pin with a small package; less than two minutes after the final bell the show went off air with a heavily bloodied Funk celebrating in the crowd next to John 'Hat Guy' Bailey.

The reason for the rush at the finish was not just that there were only a few minutes of satellite time left: the power generator necessary to run a live broadcast from such an unlikely venue either exploded ten seconds after the show finished, or would have cut out several minutes later, depending on how elaborately the story is told. Either way, the disaster of losing the signal early was averted, and all that remained was for the wrestlers to come to the ring and hold Heyman aloft as the tears and beers flowed.

The test of putting together a well-produced show that was controlled but still true to the ECW style had been passed, but attention soon turned to financial matters. The overnight estimates of 20,000 to 35,000 buys were considered acceptable, so it was more than satisfying when the final figures settled in the 40,000 to 45,000 range. This was equivalent to 0.26% of the potential audience, a buyrate around half that achieved by the month's respective shows from WWF and WCW (though these did three to four times the numbers of buys because they were available on all the major cable systems). Indeed, because a disproportionate number of homes not receiving the show were in ECW's main northeastern market, it is likely that had Viewers Choice carried the show, Barely Legal would have broken even or even turned a profit.

One critic rated the show two or three out of ten for match quality and ring psychology and nine or ten for highspots, stiffness and emotion, adding "I am surprised, quite frankly, that it did as well as it did. I think Paul Heyman and everyone at ECW should be proud of what they have accomplished and should be congratulated for succeeding in spite of all the adversity and obstacles that were in their way."

Yes, even Eric Bischoff had a good word to say about Barely Legal.

16: Anatomy of a feud – Raven vs Dreamer

"So it is written, and so it shall come to pass." (Raven)

1994

16 December: Stevie Richards wrestles at a TV taping under the name Stevie The Body.

17 December: Stevie Richards wrestles at Holiday Hell under the name Stevie Flamingo.

27 December: Joey Styles announces on TV that Scotty the Body/Flamingo/Johnny Polo is now working as a roadie for Stone Temple Pilots.

1995

3 January: Richards' two match win streak ends in a loss to Tommy Dreamer (taped at the 16 December show)

7 January: Richards introduces Scott Levy as his manager, Raven, at the ECW Arena. When the incident airs on TV, Joey Styles explains Raven's demeanor by saying "He's been through a traumatic experience and from what I'm told, working for the WWF will do that to a person." Richards is portrayed as a pitiful lackey: where Raven wears a Ministry shirt, Richards wears Winger (a gag possibly borrowed from the Stuart character in *Beavis & Butthead*), and where Raven wears knee-length cut-off jeans, Richards wears Daisy Duke-style denim shorts. (The leader-flunky relationship is mirrored in real life.)

17 January: The TV show airs with a video package, set to Offspring's *Come Out And Play*, featuring Raven wandering aimlessly in snow-filled streets. Raven then speaks of how he is part of a lost generation.

4 February: Dreamer pins Richards at ECW Arena. Raven and Dreamer engage in a staredown after the match.

25 February: Raven introduces Tony Stetson and Johnny Hotbody as his henchman, hired to take out Dreamer. Dreamer attacks all four men with a road sign.

18 March: Dreamer faces Raven in a 'Generation X' Gauntlet match at the ECW Arena where Dreamer must beat three opponents before getting to Raven. Dreamer overcomes Stetson, Hotbody & Richards. Raven, who has been handcuffed to the cornerpost to prevent him interfering, immediately decks Dreamer with the cuffs and DDTs him on the concrete floor, before rolling him into the ring for the pin in 25 seconds, leaving him a bloody mess.

4 April: In a TV interview, Dreamer claims Raven would leave ECW if he got a better offer, while Dreamer will stay with ECW no matter what.

8 April: At the ECW Arena, Richards reveals that Raven and Dreamer were at summer camp together as teenagers. He introduces another ex-camper, the then overweight and ugly Beulah McGillicutty. Beulah has bloomed into a beautiful, slender woman. Raven faces Dreamer in a match ending with Beulah spraying hairspray in Dreamer's eyes at ringside and Richards superkicking the blinded Dreamer into a Raven DDT on the concrete, leading to the easy pin. On the same show, Raven tells Stetson and Hotbody that they must beat the Pitbulls or be fired. When the Pitbulls win in less than a minute, Raven announces they now work for him.

14 April: Dreamer pins Raven at Jim Thorpe, Pennsylvania. *This match is never referred to during the rest of the feud, the central point of which is that Dreamer has never pinned Raven.*

15 April: Dreamer faces Raven at the ECW Arena and uses a hockey stick and a Godzilla figure among other weapons. Dreamer is disqualified for DDTing the referee, but gains some revenge by piledriving Beulah.

28 April: Dreamer pins Raven at Mifflintown, Pennsylvania. *This match, like the one on 14 April, is ignored in the mythology of the feud.*

5 May: Raven pins Dreamer in Fort Lauderdale, Florida thanks to interference from Richards. After the match, Luna Vachon attacks Raven, Dreamer piledrivers Beulah, and Luna and Dreamer kiss.

6 May: Raven pins Dreamer in Tampa, Florida.

9 May: The TV show airs clips of ECW wrestlers partying at a Florida nightclub. Raven attacks Dreamer and the pair brawl through the club. (Nursing a concussion from a match earlier in the night, Mikey Whipwreck has forgotten the angle is being shot and has no idea why the pair are brawling.)

13 May: Raven & Richards beat Dreamer & Whipwreck when debuting referee Bill Alfonso disqualifies Dreamer for using a closed fist. On the same show, Public Enemy beat the Pitbulls to earn five minutes in the ring against Richards. The 'match' ends with Raven, Dreamer, Beulah and Luna running in for a brawl ending with Dreamer piledriving Beulah.

17 May: The TV show airs a recap of the feud to Nirvana's *Smells Like Teen Spirit.*

20 May: Cactus Jack & Dreamer beat Raven & Sandman in Langhorne, Pennsylvania, but the finish is Cactus pinning Sandman.

30 May: Speaking on the TV show, Joey Styles claims Raven and Luna were lovers during their WWF spell.

9 June: Raven & Richards beat Cactus & Dreamer in Drexel University, Philadelphia. After the match, Raven DDTs Dreamer.

17 June: At the ECW Arena Beulah pins Luna in seconds after Richards hits Luna with a chair at the opening bell. Raven DDTs Luna after the match. Dreamer makes the save, but Raven holds him down and breaks several of his fingers. Earlier on the same show, Richards introduces Luna's former husband, the Vampire Warrior (later WWF's Gangrel), but he is pinned by Dreamer.

20 June: On a TV interview, Raven explains that the physical pain he causes to Dreamer eases his own mental anguish.

30 June: Raven & Richards beat Public Enemy to win the ECW tag titles at Jim Thorpe, Pennsylvania.

1 July: In the opening match of the ECW Arena show (Pitbulls vs debuting Dudley Boys), a woman at ringside holds up a "Kiss me Stevie" sign and Richards meets her request, to Beulah's annoyance. Raven drags Beulah and Richards backstage; the distraction causes a loss for the Pitbulls. The Pitbulls complain to Joey Styles that Raven is not watching their back. Later in the show, Raven & Richards beat Dreamer & Luna after Beulah throws powder in Luna's eyes. After the following match, Luna challenges Richards to a future cage match. Richards comes out to accept, but a brawl breaks out with Raven and Dreamer. The Pitbulls come out and attack Richards and Raven, but the Dudley's come to Raven's defence.

4 July: In a TV interview, the goofy Richards celebrates his tag title win with a rendition of *We Are The Champions* and a karate-style dance.

15 July: Raven & Richards lose an ECW Arena match against Stetson & Don E Allen by countout after Raven goes to ringside to break up a smooch between Richards and his female admirer. Beulah and the mystery woman fight, prompting a mass brawl with the Pitbulls, Dreamer and Dudleys. When things settle down, Stetson and Allen celebrate their win, prompting Raven to attack them, leading to another mass brawl with everyone involved. Later in the show Dreamer & the Pitbulls beat Raven & the Dudleys (a Pitbull pins a Dudley), with Luna interfering to attack Raven. In a later match, Luna beats Richards inside a cage when she grabs his testicles for a submission. In a familiar pattern, Raven, Dreamer, the Pitbulls and the Dudleys break into the cage for another brawl, ending with Raven handcuffed to the cage, and Dreamer hitting him in the head with a chair, a move so forceful it is dubbed 'the chairshot heard around the world'.

20 July: Raven & Richards beat Dreamer & Luna in Fort Lauderdale, Florida. After a Pitbulls match later in the night, a mass brawl develops with the Pitbulls, Raven, Richards, Dreamer, Luna, Dudley Dudley and Vampire Warrior.

21 July: Raven & Richards beat Dreamer & Luna in Tampa, Florida. After the match the Pitbulls, Dudley Dudley and Vampire Warrior hit the ring for another brawl.

22 July: Raven beats Dreamer in Orlando. Florida.

25 July: In a TV interview with Raven filmed on a beach, Richards glances at Beulah and spoofs *Apocalypse Now* with the memorable line "I love the smell of fish in the morning".

5 August: Raven, Richards & the Dudleys beat Dreamer, Cactus & the Pitbulls at the ECW Arena when Raven pins Dreamer after Cactus turns heel and becomes a follower of Raven.

26 August: Beulah beats Richards' female admirer (now

named Francine) in a cat fight. Richards is the guest referee, but superkicks Francine to show his support for Raven.

16 September: The Pitbulls beat Raven & Richards in a double dog collar match at ECW Arena to win the tag titles. Dreamer replaces Pitbull #2 midway through the match and scores his 'first' pin on Raven, but heel referee Bill Alfonso overturns the decision because Dreamer is not the legal man.

7 October: Raven interferes in a Cactus Jack match, prompting Dreamer to come out to make the save. The ensuing fight sees Dreamer stretchered from the ring.

17 October: The TV show recaps the Raven-Dreamer rivalry to Nirvana's *Heart Shaped Box*.

27 October: Raven pins Dreamer in Kennet Square, Pennsylvania. Both men interfere in a Cactus Jack vs Konnan match, as do Richards, the Dudleys and 911.

28 October: Raven is in Cactus' corner for his match at the ECW Arena with Dreamer. The match ends in a no-contest and the arena lights go out; when they come back on, Raven has Dreamer 'crucified' on a balcony. Unfortunately most of the crowd are distracted by a flaming chair having got out of control and burned a ringside fan.

November: Beulah appears nude in the hardcore porn magazine *Cherie*. This has no direct effect on storylines, but does stir certain emotions among the ECW fanbase.

17 November: Raven, Sandman, Too Cold Scorpio, Cactus & Richards beat Dreamer, The Pitbulls, & The Public Enemy in a 'rumble games' elimination match.

18 November: Dreamer & Terry Funk beat Raven & Cactus at the ECW Arena, but it is Funk who pins Raven.

21 November: In a TV interview, Raven 'reveals' that when he was 16 his parents divorced, and summer camp friend Dreamer was not there for him.

25 November: Raven pins Dreamer in Salisbury, Massachusetts.

1 December: Raven and Dreamer brawl during post-match chaos after a Dudleys-Public Enemy match.

9 December: Dreamer, Public Enemy & the Pitbulls beat

Raven, the Heavenly Bodies, the Eliminators & Richards in an 'Ultimate Jeopardy' cage match where each person faced a particular forfeit for losing. Had Raven lost, whomever pinned him would get Beulah for a week. Had Dreamer lost, his head would have been shaved. In the event, Richards loses and faces five minutes alone with the other team. However, Raven has handcuffed the Pitbulls and Public Enemy to the cage, and he and Richards spend the five minutes beating down Dreamer, concluding with a DDT on a chair.

28 December: Dreamer & Whipwreck beat Raven & Richards in Glenolden, Pennsylvania, but it is Richards who is pinned.

30 December: Raven pins Dreamer in Queens, New York. The winner would face Sandman for the title later in the night, and many fans wrongly assumed Dreamer would win to set up a face vs heel bout.

1996

6 January: At the ECW Arena, Richards boasts about being kissed by Missy Hyatt at the Queens show. He attempts to steal a kiss from Beulah, but she pushes him aside and reveals she is pregnant. Raven berates her for forgetting to take the pill, but she tells him it's not his baby. As Raven furiously attacks Richards, Beulah reveals that it's not his baby either: It's Dreamer's. Dreamer hits the ring and attacks Raven, Richards, and Richards' flunky the Blue Meanie. The assault climaxes with Dreamer grabbing a sign from Sign Guy requesting "Tommy: Use my sign!" Dreamer smashes Raven over the head with it, then tears the cardboard apart to reveal a street sign underneath. Dreamer leaves the ring with Beulah.

27 January: Raven beats Sandman for the ECW title at the ECW Arena despite interference by Dreamer. Raven is now accompanied by a Hawaiian-looking woman named Kimona Wanaleia.

2 February: Dreamer & Shane Douglas beat Raven & Richards in Reading, Pennsylvania, but the finish is Douglas pinning Richards.

3 February: Dreamer & Douglas beat Raven & Richards in

Queens, New York, but Dreamer pins Richards.

17 February: At the ECW Arena, Raven and company interrupt a Dreamer interview. On Raven's orders, the Bruise Brothers ram Dreamer crotch-first into the ring post.

27 February: In a TV interview, Raven points out that in some countries a thief will have his hand cut off, and at one time a liar would have his tongue cut out. He explains that the attack by the Bruise Brothers followed similar logic.

9 March: At the ECW Arena, Raven beats Douglas to retain the title. After the match the Bruise Brothers attempt to put Douglas crotch-first into the post. Dreamer makes the save, but they attempt to do the same to him. Sandman makes the save, but he and Dreamer argue over who should have the right to attack Raven.

30 March: Dreamer, Sandman & Douglas beat Raven & the Bruise Brothers at the ECW Arena, but it is Douglas who pins Raven. Earlier in the show a brawl involving all six men sees Brian Lee debut and join the assault on Dreamer.

13 April: During a six-man tag in Queens, New York, with Lee & the Bruise Brothers vs Dreamer & Pitbulls, Raven appears at ringside and DDTs Dreamer, leading to him being pinned.

20 April: At the ECW Arena Douglas reveals that Beulah is not really pregnant. Beulah admits she has been cheating on Dreamer. When he asks Beulah "Who is he?", Douglas says "It's not a he." Kimona grabs the microphone and says "It's me!" before kissing Beulah. Dreamer kisses both women and claims that he is hardcore enough to take both. He later interferes in a Raven vs Douglas title match.

31 May: In a TV interview Raven claims he only brought Kimona to ECW because he knew she was having an affair with Beulah and having her around meant he was with Beulah in spirit. He asks Richards to bring him the most pathetic woman he can find to get over the loss of Kimona.

1 June: At the ECW Arena, Richards brings out Hollywood street prostitute Divine Brown (known for her dalliance with Hugh Grant). Raven refuses to accept her because she hasn't been with enough men. Later in the show, Dreamer & the Pitbulls face Lee & the Bruise Brothers. Raven appears on the arena stage and DDTs

Dreamer to set up a Lee chokeslam through two tables.

14 June: Raven beats Dreamer in Jim Thorpe, Pennsylvania.

22 June: Following Raven's win over the debuting Terry Gordy, Dreamer DDTs Raven.

12 July: Dreamer & Gordy beat Raven & Lee in Allentown, Pennsylvania.

13 July: Dreamer, Sandman & Gordy beat Raven, Richards & Lee when Sandman pins Raven.

10 August: Dreamer & Gordy beat Raven & Richards in Yokohama, Japan when Dreamer pins Richards.

11 August: Raven pins Dreamer in Tokyo, Japan.

13 September: Dreamer & Sandman beat Raven & Lee in Jim Thorpe. Pennsylvania.

27 September: Raven attacks Dreamer after he beats Lee in Allentown, Pennsylvania.

5 October: Sandman & Dreamer are scheduled to meet Raven & Lee in an 'Ultimate Jeopardy' match at the ECW Arena, with Raven's belt at stake if he lost. Raven misses the show (having gone into drug rehab) and Sandman pins replacement Richards to capture the title.

26 October: Raven returns from rehab, caning Sandman at the ECW Arena.

1 November: Dreamer & Sandman beat Raven & Lee in Staten Island, New York when Sandman pins Raven.

15 November: Dreamer & Sandman beat Raven & Richards in Plymouth Meeting, Pennsylvania

7 December: Raven beats Sandman in a barbed wire match to regain the title.

1997

17 January: Dreamer & Pitbull 2 beat Douglas & Raven at the Tabor Youth Center in Philadelphia.

31 January: Dreamer & Sandman beat Raven & Richards in Lake Grove, New York when Sandman pins Raven.

14 February: Dreamer & Sandman beat Raven & Richards in Webster, Massachusetts when Sandman pins Raven.

15 February: Dreamer & The Pitbulls beat Raven, Lee & Candido in Revere, Massachusetts.

21 February: Dreamer & Sandman beat Raven & Richards in Queens, New York when Sandman pins Raven.

22 February: Dreamer & Funk beat Raven & Lee at the ECW Arena. A match stipulation says that if Funk pinned Raven, he would get a future title shot. At the start of the match, Raven lays down and offers to let Dreamer pin him for the 'first' time, but at the expense of Funk's title shot. Dreamer declines. The match ends in chaos with Sandman somehow scoring the pin on Raven and reuniting with his son, while Richards breaks up with Raven and shakes hands with Dreamer.

15 March: Raven is schedule to team with a mystery partner at the ECW Arena against Dreamer & Richards. A female fan who has previously attacked Richards at ringside is invited to draw the name of Raven's partner and somehow draws Richards. The match is changed to a three way dance and, after interference from at least 17 people, Raven pins Richards. The woman extends her arms into a crucifix pose to show she is allied with Raven, so Dreamer piledrives her. The woman is later named Chastity.

21 March: As Dreamer, Funk and Sandman argue with one another in Waltham, Massachusetts, Raven appears at ringside but walks away rather than fight.

29 March: Raven is scheduled to face Sandman in New Kensington, Pennsylvania, but Brian Lee attacks Sandman before the match. Dreamer comes out to make the save but is beaten down by Lee.

30 March: Raven & Douglas beat Funk & Dreamer in Monaco, Pennsylvania when Raven pins Dreamer.

5 April: Funk & Dreamer beat Raven & Douglas in Queens, New York when Dreamer pins Douglas.

13 April: During a Raven vs Funk match at Barely Legal, Dreamer DDTs Raven, leading to him losing the title to Terry Funk.

17 May: Raven & Richards beat Dreamer & Funk in Buffalo, New York when Richards pins Funk.

6 June: Despite interference from Lupus (a new Raven lackey), Chasity and Louie Spicolli, Dreamer pins Raven in a loser-leaves-ECW match at the ECW Arena. While not, as claimed, his first pinfall over Raven, it is the first time Dreamer has pinned him in 38 straight matches involving the pair, ending a two and a half year feud... for the time being.

17: ECW vs WWF

"An ECW fan will actually buy a ticket to a WWF show, see an ECW wrestler on there and tell him that he *sold out... when they've just paid to see him!" (Rob Van Dam,* PowerSlam *magazine)*

The Raven-Dreamer bout was just one part of a forty-plus minute series of matches and angles which highlighted the WrestlePalooza '97 show. Only a few seconds after the match ended, the arena lights went out, coming back on to reveal Rob Van Dam and Alfonso attacking Dreamer. A second lighting malfunction led to Sabu joining the assault (while hiding Raven's departure from the ring, and the company), and a third blackout produced the debuting Jerry Lawler. The trio beat off all-comers, including Heyman, The Gangstas and Sandman, until Taz single-handedly cleared the ring. This led directly to the Sabu-Taz rematch, with Sabu scoring the pin despite being held in the katahajime submission. Following this bout, Taz began exchanging words with Shane Douglas (who had watched the entire Lawler angle from the main stage and refused to come to the company's aid), ending in a challenge for Taz to beat Douglas within three minutes or leave the company for 60 days. Two minutes and fifty seconds later, there was a new TV champion. The whole sequence was yet another example of the Heyman booking technique of putting together a series of feuds to produce a greater whole.

The Lawler appearance was a surprise, but followed logically from recent events involving Van Dam. Although his push as 'Mr Monday Night' had begun with rumours of a post-Barely Legal departure to WCW, he had a surprise up his sleeve. After an ECW match on 12 May he guaranteed he would be wrestling on the following Monday. Only it was *RAW* where he made his appearance, defeating a young jobber named Jeff Hardy and explaining to commentator Jerry Lawler that "ECW is all low-budget wannabes who can't compete with the extreme talents of Rob Van Dam". On the following week's ECW TV he was "suspended" (a cover story for an All Japan tour) and most of the roster gave interviews condemning his actions. Ironically what had started as rumours based on reality were now purely storyline, with Van Dam's WWF appearance part of a continuing angle between the two companies.

An aspect of the feud that is largely forgotten is that it also stretched to Memphis. On the morning of WrestlePalooza, Lawler ran down ECW on the USWA TV show, with Dreamer responding by videotape. Two days later, Van Dam was on *RAW* again, beating Flash Funk, as well as taping a match for the weekend *Shotgun* show where he teamed with Lawler to beat the Headbangers; both matches saw Tommy Dreamer interfering. On the following Saturday Dreamer destroyed the Memphis studio, while the next episode of RAW had an inter-promotional match with Chris Candido against Brian Christopher, Lawler interfering after slapping guest commentator Paul Heyman for revealing that Christopher was his son. On the same show, the Headbangers got revenge against Lawler & Van Dam after Sandman swung his cane in Lawler's family jewels.

The *RAW* end of the angle came to a hasty end the following week. Not only did Sabu upset WWF officials by running into the crowd without warning after defeating Flash Funk (the former Too Cold Scorpio), but Van Dam refused to wrestle Jesse Jammes (Brian 'Road Dogg' Armstrong) after being told he would lose by countout, his reasoning being that he was too big a star to lose to a midcarder. The issue caused rumours of a genuine rift between the two promotions, particularly when Heyman told fans in New York that "For those of you who think Vince McMahon has one dime in the company: Hey Vince, fuck you, fuck you, and stop fucking Bruce Prichard up the fucking ass!" However, he was largely telling the fans what they wanted to hear (taking particular care with his description of the financial relationship with the WWF), and a meeting with McMahon at Titan Towers smoothed out the genuine problems. Indeed, clips from Steve Austin's run in ECW appeared as part of the newly-released *'Cause Stone Cold Said So* video; talk of Joey Styles suing the WWF for unauthorised use of his voice appeared to be part of the angle.

Back in Philadelphia rings, though, the feud was still well and truly on. During a Van Dam and Sabu vs Dreamer and Sandman match, the lights again went out, with Lawler in the ring when they came back on. A second flick of the lightswitch revealed a tennis racket-swinging Jim Cornette who, to put it mildly, was no friend of Heyman. (The pair had fallen out during Heyman's WCW run, while Cornette was vocal in his dislike of the ECW product, though Chris Candido, who worked for both, theorised that the pair were more similar than either realised. In any case, this was strictly a one-night deal set up by, of all people, Dennis Coraluzzo.) During the brawl, Lawler caned Dreamer in the groin so hard that he was legitimately taken to hospital to have blood drained from his testicles.

So heated was the crowd response, Cornette's mouth was bloodied when he was hit with a drinks can, and another object hit him in the back of the head. The angle ended with Taz clearing the ring and then confronting a fan who was bravely or foolishly wearing a *WWF RAW* shirt. The fan refused to take it off, with Taz praising his courage but pointing out that the crowd might force him to remove it; as those nearby began putting their hands on him, the fan took Taz' advice and handed the shirt over, with Taz placing it on a chair in the middle of the ring and symbolically setting it ablaze.

In the following Arena show's main event, Lawler, Van Dam and Sabu took on Sandman and Dreamer plus a mystery partner in a cage match. Said partner turned out to be Rick Rude, who was at the time working as Styles' broadcast partner on the TV show. Given that Rude had retired because of a serious back injury, he was never going to be the best of partners, but things turned worse when he immediately clotheslined Dreamer and left he and Sandman to fend for themselves.

The main thrust of the feud climaxed as Dreamer faced Lawler at the second ECW pay-per-view, Hardcore Heaven. Held in Fort Lauderdale, it received strong reviews from the near-2000 in attendance, but on television it was hurt by atrocious production, with poor lighting and audio problems. The show also featured a series of skits with Sandman taken to hospital, hijacking the ambulance and driving back to the arena (stopping to buy beer), accompanied by live coverage from a helicopter by Lance Wright. The routine was meant to spoof two similar incidents on WCW shows, but most viewers didn't get the reference and saw it as bush league.

Inside the ring, Dreamer beat Lawler after surprise interference from Rude, Jake Roberts and the WWF's Sunny. Other matches included the Dudleys (accompanied by hardcore porn star

Jenna Jameson) beating the USWA's PG-13, and Van Dam beating Al Snow, on long-term loan from the WWF. The main event was a rematch of the famous three-way with Douglas, Terry Funk and new ECW champion Sabu, who had won the title in a brutal barbed wire match at the ECW Arena a week earlier in which his arm was literally ripped apart. He had simply taped it back in place and finished the match before getting stitches. (The decision to show clips of the bout on TV quickly ended negotiations for a slot on the Sports Channel station in the potentially lucrative Chicago market.) Despite interference in the Hardcore Heaven bout from Sandman and Dory Funk Jr, Douglas regained the title, with the broadcast ending with a huge brawl dominated by new makeshift tag team New Jack and Kronus.

At this point the new pairing was only necessary because of injuries (in Saturn's case, a seriously broken leg and kneecap), but within two weeks Saturn shockingly signed with WCW. And he wasn't alone. Raven had departed in June with the news widely leaked beforehand, making it even more impressive when fans bought some of his pin attempts in the farewell match against Dreamer. Steve Richards had followed a few weeks later, having suffered a sprained neck and been advised by a doctor that the ECW style was no longer for him. Though Heyman had advised him that if he was going to leave, he should try the WWF, he instead debuted on WCW TV without giving notice, causing resentment along colleagues. The heat between ECW and WCW increased when Raven appeared on the Bash at the Beach pay-per-view, breaching his ECW contract which did not allow him to appear on such a show until six months after Barely Legal. Threats of legal action came to nothing, apparently because the costs of pursuing a claim were too extravagant when there would likely be little or nothing to gain; there was also some dispute over whether the restriction applied to any appearance, or specifically an in-ring match.

However, the departure of Saturn was even more controversial. Shortly after he signed, speculation began running rampant that a 'mole' was trying to betray ECW and take a group of wrestlers to WCW. It's not clear who floated the story (WCW to damage the company, or ECW to cast themselves as the wronged party), but within a few days Joey Styles was talking about the issue on the ECW hotline and promising to name the mole on his next update. But a day before that update, the name got out... it was Tod Gordon.

According to Gordon, he was planning to leave the company to spend more time with his family. At a show in Trenton on 23 August (the week after Hardcore Heaven), he was talking to Sabu, Van Dam, Alfonso, Saturn and Sandman, all of whom were disgruntled with the direction of the company. (By this point, there was underlying tension between this group of wrestlers and those allied with Heyman, such as Taz, Tommy Dreamer and the Dudleys). Gordon approached WCW on their behalf to offer a package deal by which the group would sign (other accounts add New Jack and The Pitbulls to the list) and 'invade' the company. Gordon would not accompany the group, but would receive a healthy payoff for setting the deal up.

Terry Taylor began discussing the deal, with the hold-up being that WCW did not necessarily want everyone involved (Sabu's past WCW run, New Jack's reputation, and the potential bad publicity from the Pitbulls, who had recently been dropped by ECW after being charged with drug trafficking, were all potential problems) and preferred to negotiate individually, no doubt looking to get each man for as little as possible. It's widely believed that Kevin Sullivan leaked news of the negotiations to Heyman, who immediately began asking questions and looking to sign more wrestlers to contracts. Eventually the negotiations broke down and only Saturn, who was confronted directly by Heyman, made the jump. Meanwhile Alfonso was apparently the only person to directly lie about the talks and was close to being fired but, so the story goes, saved his job with his bloody performance in a match with Beulah McGillicutty at the next Arena show.

Whether Gordon was fired or quit is open to debate, though he claims Heyman suggested turning the incident into an angle, but Gordon was no longer willing to work shows outside of Philadelphia. Either way, Gordon was going and, probably because a public slanging match would do neither man any good, Heyman went on TV and announced he had accepted Gordon's resignation to concentrate on his family and business. The idea that it was a firing is backed by

Gabe Sapolsky, who worked in the ECW office above the Carver W Reed store (at one point assisted by Richards under the false name 'Lloyd Van Buren'), being told by Heyman to clear out his belongings, a couple of days before Gordon's departure. The ECW office phoneline was transferred to Sapolsky's apartment, with a physical office eventually being set up in the New York warehouse that stored the company's merchandise and being staffed during the day by Little Guido. Dreamer took on many of the day-to-day business roles, while Bubba Ray Dudley (now spelt that way) took charge of booking arenas.

The changes came as business continued to grow. During the year the promotion ran 98 shows (up from 67 the year before), with several three-day swings. As well as the Arena shows, they were now running Queens and Fort Lauderdale every month, with several other venues running regular dates every other month. Perhaps the most notable house show came on Hallowe'en night in Stamford, Connecticut, home of the WWF, with wrestlers such as Snow (Avatar), Chris Candido (Skip), Douglas (Dean Douglas) and Justin Credible (Aldo Montoya) all donning their former gimmicks in what was billed as the ultimate horror.

The company broke its attendance record during the summer with a show in Buffalo, New York drawing 1,697; similar or larger crowds had been claimed for the ECW Arena, but close examination of photographs and video of events in that era show the company was barely (if at all) exceeding the fire department's legal limit for the building of 1,080. There was no disputing the record when a show at Monaca, Pennsylvania attracted 1,926 fans, with a later show in the building drawing 2,200. Almost half the shows during the year broke the 1,000 barrier, with barely a handful falling below the 500 mark.

And the record was shattered by the third pay-per-view, November to Remember, again at the Golden Dome in Monaca where, thanks in part to strong local promotion by Shane Douglas, 4,634 were on hand to see him regain the ECW title (having dropped it to Bam Bam Bigelow in Queens a month earlier). Early matches on the show such as Candido vs Tommy Rogers turning into a tag match with Lance Storm and Jerry Lynn, Mikey Whipwreck ending Justin Credible's televised undefeated streak, Taz squashing Pitbull 2 (now managed by 'WWF loyalist' Lance Wright) and a four way tag brawl went down well. Most people's pick for match of the night was Van Dam vs Dreamer in a flag match (ECW vs WWF banners rather than national colours) with widespread interference from the likes of Doug Furnas and Phil 'Dan Kroffat' LaFon (under WWF contract but on 'developmental' loan) and the surprise return of Richards leading to a disappointing no contest. The disappointment continued with Sabu against Sandman in a match where everything that could go wrong did, followed by the main event title match which, though competent, went too long to hold the crowd's attention.

Although the buyrate fell slightly from that of the company's first two shows, the revenue was healthier thanks to Viewers Choice responding to continued pressure from fans (particularly the 'Simply ECW' group led by Tony Lewis) by carrying the event on its secondary 'Hot Choice' network, more commonly used for pornographic movies. The apparent contradiction of the product becoming less consistent but revenues continuing to rise would become a running theme as the company entered 1998.

18: 1998

"Where would the WWF and WCW be today if it wasn't for Paul E Dangerously and hardcore wrestling? [They've] copied everything he's done. They did it so much that it's damaged ECW. (Terry Funk, PowerSlam)

ECW had always been the place where the most skilled but underused wrestlers went to perform to the best of their ability. Al Snow & Lance Storm vs Chris Candido & Shane Douglas should have been a dream pay-per-view main event, perhaps half an hour of state-of-the-art grappling. Instead, it went less than five minutes, took place in a ring where one section was cordoned off with police tape, and saw all four attempt to work in a sea of Styrofoam heads. Something was up.

Snow was one of the main creative successes of the period, the only notable benefit of the WWF's developmental arrangement by which, as well as paying ECW a weekly fee, they paid the salaries and transport costs of WWF contracted wrestlers on ECW shows, in return for the rights to any successful characters created for them. Doug Furnas and Phil LaFon (who had been doomed in the WWF by a misguided 'gimmick' of being labelled boring) made the trip but never returned, while Darren Drozdov received a solid ECW push, even no-selling stiff weapon shots from New Jack, only to be repackaged by as a third member of the Legion of Doom on his return to the WWF. Perhaps the most successful long-term character creation was that of Justin Credible, who followed up a shock win over the Great Sasuke by holding his own in feuds with Sandman and Tommy Dreamer, also taking part in a near-the-knuckle angle when he interrupted and disrespected a ten bell ceremony for Dreamer's grandfather (who had legitimately passed away). By the end of the year, Credible's WWF contract had run out and he remained as an ECW regular with Paul Heyman fully intending to push him as the company's lead heel once they had national television.

Despite his long-standing reputation as 'the best wrestler you've never heard of', Al Snow's rise to stardom in ECW was strictly down to character and gimmick rather than his natural abilities. After an attempt to establish his mental strain by talking to himself failed to get across to the audience, he began appearing at ringside with a mannequin head (found backstage from stock used for the Mummer's Day floats) which served as his adviser. With Snow later adding the words "Help Me" written backwards to the head, and both interviews and commentary littered with fellatio puns, the character soon caught on. But the push to main event status came when the company began handing out polystyrene heads to the crowd to wave during Snow's entrance which, combined with upside-down camera angles, strobe lighting and The Prodigy's *Breathe*, created an unforgettable entrance. The only problem was that, similar to the very characters which ECW loyalists would criticise in the new-style WWF product, the interest didn't last much beyond the entrance; hence the aforementioned tag match going just 4:49 (of which, thanks to a mystery partner swerve with Sunny, Snow was in the ring for barely a minute.)

The Living Dangerously pay-per-view drew a sell-out 3,700 crowd and it appeared most fans went home happy with the show. In terms of business, it really couldn't be criticised, but thanks to the growing competition on Monday nights and the national boom in business, ECW's roster was quickly becoming regarded as 'hardest working' rather than 'most talented', while the rebranding of WWF as the 'Attitude' company, aimed firmly at the 18-34 male demographic, was beginning to hamper ECW's status as a significant alternative. And while Rob Van Dam continued to excite (defeating Too Cold Scorpio in many people's pick for match of the night), New Jack led the chaos in a wild tag team three-way, and Taz brought the big-fight atmosphere to his bout with Bam Bam Bigelow (ending with both men crashing through the ring before Bigelow took the TV belt), other aspects of the show seemed to fall into the trap of credibility-damaging hype, now without the tongue-in-cheek irony of previous years. Joey Styles' enthusiastic billing of Doug Furnas and Masato Tanaka's star status in Japan was criticised (particularly after the pair's bout fell flat to say the least), while the publicity that a Sabu vs Sandman match had to be pre-taped in case it was too extreme to broadcast only raised false expectations and drew attention to the more likely reason that they didn't dare put the pair on live television for fear of repeating the November to Remember debacle. Yet with the addition of Time Warner to the networks carrying the show, bringing ECW to 90% of homes, the show was the highest-drawing to date. And having lost $1.2 million dollars in 1997, increased revenue was vital for the company.

While the merits of Living Dangerously could at least be debated, there were few praising the second show of 1998, WrestlePalooza. By this stage, fears that the ECW style could not hold up to regular three-show swings without injury problems were starting to look well founded. In the run-up to the show, Sandman suffered neck problems thanks to a Dudley 3D (Dudley Death Drop) finisher and a cane shot, Taz cut his calf muscle while going through a table, Furnas injured his throat, and Douglas, already suffering elbow problems, injured bones in the roof of his mouth, leading to his sinuses exploding during a flight. In the main event, Douglas retained the title against Snow in just 13 minutes, despite needing surgery on his elbow which would require him to take the summer off to recover. (Heyman kept the title on him throughout his absence, feeling it was more important to protect the lineage of the title than to have an active champion). Snow, whose gimmick had largely run its course, would return to the WWF a few weeks later, responding to the ECW Arena crowd's chants of "You sold out" with an angry "From the bottom of my heart, fuck you all."

Furnas and Taz both missed the show with their injuries, while Sandman was hidden in a six-man tag. Elsewhere Tommy Dreamer and Mikey Whipwreck both showed signs of serious wear and tear, while New Jack collapsed midway through his match with Bam Bam Bigelow and was literally dragged by security staff to a balcony to perform a dive, then dragged by Bigelow to the ring to be pinned. (New Jack was also involved in a backstage incident when he attempted to collect an unpaid debt from Junk Yard Dog, who was introduced as a guest legend.) And the most memorable moment of a spectacular but directionless thirty minute draw between Van Dam and Sabu came when the latter vomited live on camera. At this point it seemed the only thing ECW could lead the industry in was effort, and that was no longer a guarantee of entertainment.

Again, the irony was that however poorly the show might

have come across compared to previous company efforts, it was another financial success. As well as drawing nearly 3,500 fans live (and breaking the per head merchandise sales record for any promotion's show in US history), it was the most successful pay-per-view to date thanks to Viewers Choice now carrying the show on its main station. And another successful campaign by Strictly ECW persuaded Cablevision to become the last major provider to pick up the show.

The goal of achieving a financially successful *and* critically acclaimed show finally came to fruition with HeatWave, held before 5,376 fans (of whom just under 4,000 paid). Justin Credible beat Jerry Lynn and Chris Candido beat Lance Storm in two more-than-competent openers. Masato Tanaka beat Mike Awesome in what would become their signature high-impact style of match. Sabu & Van Dam beat Jinsei Shinzaki (formerly Hakushi) and Hayabusa in what was the best or worst match of the evening depending on your stylistic preferences. Taz, now wearing his self-created 'Fuck The World' championship belt (effectively declaring himself top dog during Douglas' absence) got revenge on Bigelow, the pair this time crashing through the entrance rampway. And the main event had Dreamer, Sandman and Spike Dudley over Bubba, D Von and Big Dick in a well-packaged brawl.

But what would a couple of years earlier be considered business as usual turned out to be a one-off critical success. The follow-up November to Remember pay-per-view reverted back to the now-familiar status of being inconsistent in all facets except hard work. The main event, a six-man with the latest Triple Threat incarnation of Douglas, Candido and Bigelow against Van Dam, Sabu and Taz was intended to climax with the first face-off between Douglas and Taz in well over a year. Unfortunately timing errors meant the crowd's attention was distracted by an abortive attempt by Van Dam to dive into the crowd onto Bigelow. And the finish, intended to be Taz putting Douglas in the katahajime but Sabu landing an Arabian facebuster (a legdrop holding onto a chair) on both men and 'stealing' the pin, came off without the intended ambiguity when Sabu clearly only hit Douglas. Elsewhere Storm and Lynn had the match of the night despite the emphasis being on a scantily clad Tammy Fytch (Sunny) as referee. The rest of the undercard was littered with unadvertised clusters, including a surprise appearance by Mabel who, thankfully, fell prey to a Spike Dudley Acid Drop. He was one of a series of giants to meet the same fate during 1998, including a one-night return by 911. (The PPV spot was originally scheduled for Yokozuna, but health problems meant he was banned by the state athletic commission.) And Dreamer and mystery partner Jake Roberts (a last minute replacement after negotiations with Vader fell flat) beat Credible and Jack Victory with the heavily-protected Credible having to drop the fall after intended loser Victory broke his leg.

The show still did the business at the box office, drawing a company record of 4,700 paying fans, while the pay-per-view drew a 0.23 buyrate, right in the now predictable range for the company. On the one hand it was a great achievement to continue to maintain buyrates at this level (previously only WWF, WCW and UFC had maintained success in the field despite the efforts of several other groups with impressive debut shows), but on the other it must have been disconcerting that the audience seemed to be limited to a hardcore following regardless of angles or line-ups.

And morale problems coming into the show were worsened when, as expected, Bigelow signed for WCW for what was reported to be substantially more than the $2,000 a week he was making in ECW. (At the time he left, his wife was seven months pregnant.) Despite the WWF's payments to the company, the majority of those leaving ECW were still headed to WCW which, in its biggest year ever, seemed to have no limits to its payroll. Be it miscellaneous luchadores, students of Ultimo Dragon, Power Plant training school graduates, or even a former Olympic bobsleigh competitor, it appeared anyone could get a job with the company, which seemed terrified of missing out on somebody who might instead become a WWF star.

And as with Raven, Steve Richards and Perry Saturn the year before, several of those acquisitions were not simply established stars who were passing through ECW, but rather men at the heart of the Philadelphia roster. Valet Chastity was hardly a major loss, but it was certainly surprising to see Mikey Whipwreck, by now damaged by a chronic knee injury, taking a full-time job in Atlanta. And that was nothing compared with the sight of the Sandman signing a WCW deal. Already on a healthy $150,000 a year, he 'quit' the company in August, with Heyman claiming not to be concerned, talking of putting the savings towards bringing in Chris Benoit, and booking Sandman to lose to Credible in just four minutes. While this may have been an attempt to call Sandman's bluff, Heyman was unable or unwilling to pay him any more, and a month later he signed a $200,000 a year WCW contract, the timing being particularly unfortunate as his face was the front cover of a soon-to-be released album of ECW entrance music. (The promotion was also licensing deals for action figures during this time.)

When somebody whose gimmick, style and ability seemed so rooted in ECW was tempted elsewhere by a salary increase, it was clear the Monday Night Wars were beginning to price Heyman out of the market for his own talent. And matters weren't helped by delays with receiving money from cable companies and ECW's own tight day-to-day cashflow meaning that it could take up to nine months for performers to receive their full pay-per-view bonuses (which could be equivalent to a month or more of regular pay).

As it happened, the money saved with Sandman's departure was more than outweighed by an added expenditure unconnected to the talent payroll. Throughout much of 1998 ECW's television coverage in New York was restricted to the minor PAX station after the MSG network dropped the show, with the PAX coverage dropped later in the year leaving a blackout in the city. By the end of the year ECW was back on MSG, but now as a paid 'infomercial' costing $250,000 a year. This came on top of a $150,000 a year deal to buy time in the Chicago area, which would become a major market for the company, though it was another year before they ran a show there. Elsewhere the company lost its TV outlet in Pittsburgh after the station objected to crowd chants of "Fuck New York!" and excessive blood and violence, though old tapes were picked up by Bravo in the UK. (Though there were no serious plans to run shows overseas, British stations traditionally pay for content rather than selling airtime).

During the time without TV in New York, the company handed out free tapes of the TV show to the loyal fans at the events at the Elks Lodge in Queens. Ironically, despite the lack of TV, the market was so strong that the shows there were consistently selling out. Yet even with capacity crowds, both this venue and the ECW Arena were money-losing prospects. A year earlier Heyman had told the *Pro Wrestling Torch* "As long as we can have a jam packed building and have people into what we are doing, it's better than running a big building and having empty seats. Even though we leave money on the table, I'd rather have that atmosphere because that atmosphere is worth money." While it was undoubtedly true the atmosphere transferred well to television (Queens became a regular venue for tapings), the growth in ECW's business elsewhere, and rising talent costs, was beginning to make this strategy questionable.

While the company only ran ten extra shows compared to the year before (switching to a regular three shows per week schedule in October), crowds continued to rise; almost 80% of the 108 events in 1998 attracted crowds of more than 1,000 and 18 shows broke the 2,000 mark, while early in the year a streak of 15 straight shows sold out. As part of the move to the increased schedule, the company started signing wrestlers to guaranteed weekly wages rather than per-match payoffs, but at the expense of receiving merchandise royalties (which had previously been an important top-up, particularly in weeks with only one or two shows). The company began promoting further afield, visiting Georgia, Ohio, Louisiana and Alabama for the first time, while Buffalo (boosted no doubt by the strong wrestling community just across the border in nearby Toronto), Pittsburgh and Fort Lauderdale became strong regular towns. Business was so strong that a Pittsburgh show drew 3,470 despite a second-string line-up with ten company regulars off the show for various reasons, and Douglas working despite injury. There were even plans for regular midweek gym shows in New Jersey to give younger wrestlers more ring time, the plan falling through when potential organiser Bigelow departed.

Many of the fans at these shows were attracted by the image of rowdy, violent, chaotic events, and they weren't to be disappointed. While WWF events usually got no more outrageous than crotch-chops and middle fingers, and WCW's level of anarchy involved the throwing of paper cups, stories of out-of-control scenes at ECW shows were commonplace in this era. On one show Van Dam and

Sabu were hit with flying bottles, Sabu responding by throwing a chair into the crowd and hitting a young boy in the arm. A female fan who exposed her breasts was invited into the ring by Balls Mahoney (a character who had inherited the Hack Myers "Shah/Shit" routine and adapted it to "Balls/Nuts"), causing some panic when it was unclear if she was 16 or 18, raising potential legal questions which thankfully didn't need to be answered. (The unruly atmosphere wasn't restrained to the arenas; a Pittsburgh hotel banned the entire promotion after several rooms registered to wrestlers were trashed.)

But the heart of the chaos lay with the Dudley Boys. Now the top heel act, Bubba and D Von headlined close to half the shows during the year, and were in feature matches on many of the remainder, giving credence to their case for being the best draws in company history. The pre-match microphone work by the pair paid no attention to debates about what qualified as 'cheap heat', instead doing whatever it took to work the crowds to the intended level of one step short of rioting; unfortunately the pair sometimes went the extra step. In the ring, they earned heat with attacks on a 'fan' who was in fact a relative of Beulah McGillicutty, and later delivering a 3D to Beulah herself, ending her career (in reality she was leaving the business to concentrate on college studies). Outside of storylines, one match ended with fans throwing around 30 drinks cans and 20 chairs at Bubba, provoking the combative response "We're still standing, motherfuckers!" A show in Staten Island ended with the pair inciting a chair riot among drunken fans, leading to 12 police cars arriving, and both Big Dick Dudley and a teenage fan being arrested. One fan in Poughkeepsie was idiotic enough to accept Buh Buh's now-traditional invitation to get in the ring. With fan interaction that was quite literally in-your-face, it seemed the Dudleys provided one field in which ECW truly was an alternative.

Well, that and Joel Gertner's introductions.

19: Ten classic Gertner introductions

* I'm Joel "Harder than the tree that killed Sonny Bono" Gertner

* I'm Joel "Bigger and better than the Titanic because only 400 women went down on the Titanic" Gertner

* I'm Joel "I'm like the middle of the litter box, I'm always surrounded by pussy" Gertner

* I'm Joel "The ladies call me Fred Flintstone because I make their beds rock" Gertner

* (In New Orleans) I'm Joel "A shrimp jambalaya in your Cajun all you can eat buffet of love" Gertner

* I'm Joel "Harder than Chinese algebra" Gertner

* I'm Joel "Monica Lewinsky asked me on a date and I told her 'Close but no cigar'" Gertner

* I'm Joel "Put your hands into my pocket and your eyes will pop out of their sockets" Gertner

* I'm Joel "Mark McGwire hit 70 home runs but I'm happy and set on my 69" Gertner

* Why go to the movies when you can stay home and see me, the one the ladies call *Big Daddy*, the one who already slept with *The General's Daughter* and the one who truly knows how to *Inspect-her Gadget*, I am dripping with sarcasm as your girlfriend is dripping with orgasm, for I am the quintessential studmuffin, Joel "Whether the ladies are home or here in Dayton, the girls are watching me and masturbating" Gertner.

20: Extreme Problems

"We're too small to be big, but we're too big to be small."
(Paul Heyman)

1999 kicked off with the crowning of a new champion in Taz, winning the belt from Douglas at the Guilty as Charged pay-per-view in what came across well as a 'passing the torch' big-match feel. Taz was immediately pushed as a classic NWA-style champion with the implication that he was more legitimate than the rest of the show, even going as far as challenging rival WWF and WCW champions Rock and Hulk Hogan. (No matter how exaggerated his credentials, it was a fairly safe bet that Taz would have won legitimate fights with either man at this stage.)

Despite the company's policy of protecting the heavyweight champion, though, it was clear TV champion Rob Van Dam was considered the company's biggest star. Holding the title throughout the entire year (during a near two-year reign), he headlined 49 of the company's record 128 shows during the year; the reigning heavyweight champion took top slot on just 25 occasions. This most likely had a lot to do with Van Dam's usual 20 minutes of spectacular, if inconsistent, offense being more suited to closing a show than Taz's shorter and tighter performances.

Guilty as Charged also featured a surprise appearance, a man who had been scheduled for a similar debut a year earlier before plans fell apart. For years ECW and its fanbase prided itself on promoting hard-working, under-utilised wrestlers who did not necessarily have mammoth size or an overtly muscular physique, but were willing to put their efforts into doing the best thing for the company. Sid Eudy, also known as Sid Vicious or Psycho Sid, was about as far from this characterisation as a professional wrestler could get. Indeed, more than five years earlier, Tod Gordon referred to him while making a point of principle to the *Pro Wrestling Torch*.

"There are certain people, say, for instance, Sid Vicious. Neither of these two guys [Paul Heyman and Eddie Gilbert], even if they thought Sid Vicious could draw a $100,000 house, would touch him because they respect the business. Now, I'm telling you if I told Paul, 'We could draw a $100,000 house with this guy!' he would say, 'I'm not booking him. You want to book him, that one show will be yours, but I'm not booking him.' I respect that."

It does not appear Sid directly drew any $100,000 houses for ECW, but he did receive a huge ovation from an otherwise subdued crowd at the pay-per-view. And in case anyone thought it was just the newer bandwagon-jumping fans in Kissimmee, Florida who felt this way, Sid received a similar reception at the ECW Arena the following week. On follow-up shows where Sid was not booked, fans would chant his name throughout the show, particularly when any other wrestler spoke on the microphone. Perhaps the fans had, as Mick Foley had suggested, always secretively been marks for 'star power'. Perhaps the fanbase had changed over the years. Either way, the reality that Paul Heyman was a businessman doing whatever he felt most effective to draw money was now abundantly clear to anyone who had bought into an apparent ethos that suggested anything other than profit was the priority.

Another attempt to drive revenue was a switch to six rather than four pay-per-views each year, with the price moving from $19.95 to $21.95 and then $24.95 for the Living Dangerously show in March (still $5 cheaper than the WWF and WCW alternatives). That show was headlined by Taz defeating Sabu to unify the ECW and FTW titles (having 'deliberately' lost the latter to Sabu three months earlier in a strange angle), with other bouts including Van Dam beating Jerry Lynn to kick off a lengthy feud and Douglas and Tommy Dreamer beating the new 'Impact Players' duo of Justin Credible and Lance Storm (accompanied by a 'new and improved Beulah' who was openly identified as an imposter, later being billed as 'Tammy Lynn Bytch' to feud with Tammy Sytch, and finally settling on Dawn Marie).

But the in-ring product was not the main story at this point, as a fan's sign claiming "Paul E bounced my check" highlighted. Despite business being about to peak (1999 as a whole would go down as ECW's highest revenue period), financial problems were becoming all too apparent. ECW had lost another million dollars in 1998. Pay cheques were now starting to bounce, causing serious morale problems, particularly as it appeared not everybody was affected equally, and this was happening at a time ECW was doing hot business with debut swings in Michigan and the Carolinas averaging more than 2,000 fans per show.

With cashflow the immediate problem (Heyman admitting the company was within weeks of folding), ECW took a loan from a group called Quantum Financing against the revenue from their past two pay-per-views, which they would not be receiving for another three months. Quantum paid $750,000 up front to ECW, with another $60,000 to follow when the PPV money came through, making the loan equivalent to a 16% interest charge for three months, far higher than a bank would charge. Though Heyman claimed this was simply a decision to avoid risking concrete assets (particularly new production equipment) that could threaten the company's existence, there was some speculation that the company's financial status was too woeful for a traditional bank loan, or that the company simply wasn't organised enough to provide the necessary financial documentation. (Efforts to address these problems had begun with the appointment of Steve Karel as full-time business manager in late 1998, with Gene Ciarkowski of the New Jersey Gene Boffa law firm taking the role of chief financial officer in 1999.)

To help solve the problems of cashflow with future pay-per-views, ECW took on Buena Vista television as a partner in the PPV, television ad sales and syndication elements of the business (rather than in ECW itself). Buena Vista would pay all the up front costs of putting together the pay-per-views and spend $100,000 on promotion and marketing, in return for a large cut of any increase over the existing buyrates; in the event, the buyrates barely changed. The drawback of the deal was that pay-per-view revenue payments would now go first to paying back Buena Vista's costs before ECW saw any of the money.

ECW had also sold licensing rights to video games company THQ for $100,000, but THQ had been unable to do anything with the rights because of potential conflict over a THQ deal with toy manufacturer Jakks which had its own agreement with the WWF. ECW lawyers warned THQ that the rights would be worthless if the company folded, and urged them to auction off the rights. THQ agreed to do so but insisted on taking back their initial investment and a healthy profit from the sale; ECW was so desperate for the cash that they had to agree.

And in what was touted as the latest move to save the company, ECW signed a video game deal with Acclaim, in which they received two payments of $100,000 as an advance against future royalties. This would not be the last of the dealings between the two companies.

But while there is some truth that cashflow was a major problem, particularly with the lengthy delays getting hold of pay-per-view revenue (which accounted for approximately half the company's income), the underlying issue was that ECW simply was not profitable at this point. While buyrates and house show attendance were extremely impressive for an expanding independent group, the promotion was no longer competing on the independent level. When it came to hiring talent, selling advertising and licensing, and running pay-per-views, they were now competing with WWF and WCW, with a product that was a distant third in terms of revenue. An average house show at this point had a break-even figure of 1,700 fans; while this was topped many times, there were only three occasions during company history when the monthly average was above this level. Later court figures showed that the ten highest paid performers had a combined salary equivalent to 20% of the company's gross income, compared to around 12% for the entire roster in the WWF.

In an average week during this time, ECW was taking in just short of $112,000. Simply by taking into account the total staff payroll ($74,800), the equivalent weekly cost of pay-per-view expenses ($28,800) and buying television slots in New York, Chicago, Boston and Buffalo ($9,300 total), the company would already be in the red. Add in the costs of several other stations, building hire for three shows a week, advertising, transportation costs, producing merchandise, and the general administration of running a multi-million dollar business, and the company was significantly behind the game. This was nothing new, but while the company had always survived by living month to month in the hope of eventually catching up with their debts, the increase in business meant that the numbers were bigger and it was more important than ever that all the money got into the right place at the right time. The string of deals helped stave off immediate dangers, but without a significant change, the company's continued survival was only increasing the likelihood of eventual collapse.

Balance-sheet difficulties were now beginning to translate into real-world problems. In the absence of adequate cashflow, flight costs for the roster were now being put onto some wrestlers' credit cards. Television slots in Chicago, Boston, Pittsburgh and Atlanta were either dropped to save money (the company later picking up a less prestigious timeslot on a Chicago broadcast station) or lost because of bouncing cheques, depending on who you believed, with knock-on effects on the viability of running live shows. A tour of the strong New England market had to be cancelled when the local promoter Mike Bernansky quit after a cheque to cover previous show expenses put onto a family credit card bounced, while similar problems meant the company could no longer hire their regular venue in Worcester, Massachusetts.

Other local promoters were upset when the company switched to a new deal. Previously a local promoter of an ECW show received $1 per ticket for the first 1000, and $2 for every additional ticket. Under the new system they got a flat fee between $500 and $750 up to the break-even point of 1,700 fans, and a limited bonus above this level. On the face of it, this was a far better deal for the company (previously it was possible for the promoter to make up to $2,400 on a show where the company lost money), but the new set-up meant that, for promoters in smaller buildings, there was now far less incentive to bring in the crowds.

Another attempted cost-cutting measure, cutting down on the number of wrestlers flown in to shows, got off to a poor start when an ECW Arena show had Van Dam against Skull Von Krush among the headline matches. This wasn't the only clear-cut effect of the financial problems on the in-ring product: Douglas quit the company claiming to be owed between $80,000 and $100,000, making it clear he was not returning in a speech at an independent event at the ECW Arena the day before the Hardcore Heaven pay-per-view. As a last minute solution Heyman brought back Sid (who had already quit once and no-showed events) to take Douglas' place in a match against rising heel Credible. The match ended in a disappointing two minute no contest (Heyman apparently not even considering attempting to get Sid to lay down) with both Credible and Storm coming off as minor-league nobodies; Sid only lasted one more match with ECW.

While the main body of the show was solid (another Van Dam vs Lynn bout, Storm vs Douglas, Guido vs Yoshihiro Tajiri, Super Crazy vs Taka Michinoku and The Dudleys vs Balls Mahoney and Spike Dudley), the main event was the unlikely bout of Taz successfully defending the title against Bubba Ray Dudley. The scheduled headline attraction, Taz vs Candido, was switched to a 70 second squash in the opener.

Though Candido, a tremendously gifted worker, had a similar financial dispute to Douglas causing him to leave the company for several months, Heyman had other reasons to bury him so unexpectedly. Along with Axl Rotten, Candido had earned a reputation for serious drug misuse, even beyond the wild standards of ECW. It was a poorly-kept secret that drug use and abuse was not considered the promotion's business unless it directly affected the performer's work. Konnan once described the dressing room as "Really cool, really laid back. You can smell the pot in the air. It almost smells like pot in the morning." And Tod Gordon estimated that at one point between 65 and 75% of wrestlers in the company were heavily into drugs of one kind or another. In some cases this use was purely recreational: Van Dam even appeared in a high-profile story in pro-marijuana magazine *High Times*, which briefly held-up negotiations for a national TV slot. But for a company built on a full-impact style, it was perhaps inevitable that some performers would become dependent on prescription pain medicine. In Rotten's case, what started as the prescribed four somas a day soon became 100 pills, leading to an injectable alternative named Nubain (which impaired mental and physical abilities), OxyContin, cocaine and eventually heroin.

Whether through good management or good fortune, ECW never had an active performer die in the way that afflicted both WCW and the WWF. But of those who wrestled for the company, four (Crash Holly, Louie Spicolli, Bobby Duncum Jr and Pitbull 2) later died of drug overdoses, one (Kerry Von Erich) committed suicide while facing drug charges, and four (Davey Boy Smith, Eddie

Gilbert, Terry Gordy and Road Warrior Hawk) suffered fatal heart attacks where it is at least a credible possibility that drug use was a contributing factor. Of these nine deaths among the 400 or so people who wrestled for ECW, only one came after the age of 40. In any other industry, to have one employee in 50 suffer a drug-related death within twelve years would be shocking. In professional wrestling, ECW may not have been out of the ordinary.

21: TNN

"TNN didn't want wrestlers saying 'I hate you' to their opponents. They preferred intense dislike." (Paul Heyman, The Rise And Fall Of ECW*)*

Without a national TV deal, ECW has heading for almost certain death. Signing a national TV deal proved fatal.

By 1999 it was clear that ECW's fanbase, while big enough to make pay-per-views profitable, was not generating enough money to finance a full-time promotion. The industry boom that was partly fuelled by ECW's product now meant any company competing on the national stage needed to offer wrestlers guaranteed contracts for a healthy salary. To fund this would either involve expanding the audience or better exploiting the ECW brand through merchandise and licensing deals. There was little disputing that either option would involve a single television timeslot across the country rather than a patchwork of local stations airing at whatever hour was available.

But taking such action was so imperative that ECW had little option but to sign a deal with TNN (The Nashville Network, later The National Network and now Spike TV) that proved financially disastrous. The agreement with TNN, announced on 30 June, was a three-year deal for a Friday night show, to be hosted by Joey Styles (who now quit his day job and began full-time work with the company, also becoming involved in the 1wrestling.com news site) and Joel Gertner, and produced by former *Nitro* executive Will Byrd. The contract allowed TNN to cancel at any time for any reason, but also included specific requirements such as an average 2.0 rating. There was no direct money paid either way for the show (neither ECW paying for airtime nor TNN paying a programming fee), but TNN would receive 8% of ECW's gross income for the next two and a half years, plus 10% of any profits. ECW reportedly committed to spending approximately $25,000 a week on production costs for the show, with TNN providing ECW with three minutes promotional time during the show, plus two minutes for which they could sell commercials. Based on court records of ECW's finances during this period, the company would have had to increase overall revenue by around 30% to make back the costs associated with the TNN deal, and increase revenue by just over 50% to begin turning a profit.

Despite the hopes of increased income in the future, ECW still had pressing money problems to deal with immediately. Court records show that the company was $3,172,138 in debt by September of 1999, and that production equipment, merchandise payments, back taxes and mailing expenses were all priorities for repayment, along with $240,000 in legal fees and a total of $140,000 owed to Shane Douglas, Rob Van Dam, Tommy Dreamer and Chris Candido. In the space of four days, the company took two payments of $125,000 and $625,000 from Acclaim. This brought Acclaim's total payments to ECW to a million dollars, officially a series of loans to be repaid in February 2002; in place of charging interest, Acclaim took a 15% share of the company, the first time an outsider had legally owned part of ECW. However, the exact status of what these payments represented would be disputed in future years.

With cashflow still tight, there was little money to spare for house show promotion. A four show swing in Georgia, where the company's house show debut the previous year had drawn crowds of 1,500 and 2,000, now drew an average of 500 a night. Such a spectacular drop was, at this time, a one-off situation, but in the later days of ECW the vicious circle of low advertising spending leading to smaller crowds producing less money to put back into advertising would become a major problem.

After two 'history of ECW' shows scheduled for 13 and 20 August were cancelled by mutual consent because the advertising was built around the official 27 August debut, the first TNN taping took place on 13 August in Toledo. However, Heyman was not happy with the look of the show or the crowd response and instead put a history show on the first week, and used the hot Queens crowd for the first original show, airing on 3 September. The main event of the show featured the Dudley Boys challenging for the title in what was widely known to be their farewell show before joining the WWF.

The pair had been under a verbal agreement with Vince McMahon for around a month, with Heyman encouraging them to leave, and apparently saying he was unable to give them even a one dollar pay rise. As well as this being the first high-profile example of the agreement to steer departing talent towards the WWF, Heyman may have simply decided the Dudleys' act was not suitable for the mainstream audience of TNN. Indeed, both TNN and Viewers Choice officials attending the July Heatwave pay-per-view had been upset when, as well as seeing Taz choke out Yoshihiro Tajiri with barbed wire, and the Dudleys-Spike/Balls Mahoney match involving cheese graters to the forehead and tables being set on fire, they witnessed Buh Buh launched into a foul-mouthed tirade on the fans including the less than subtle claim that "We've got some faggot in a Hawaiian shirt down here, we've got a mother in the front row who taught her daughter to suck dick, and we've got some ugly skankasaurus who's going to take nine inches of black dick so far up her ass she won't know what hit her." (TNN concerns weren't eased when the following week's TV featured an innuendo-laced speech by Joel Gertner mocking the recent death of John F Kennedy Jr in what Heyman openly admitted was a poor-taste attempt to manufacture publicity.)

The fans who 'knew' the Dudleys would be losing on their final night were shocked when they instead won the tag titles from Spike and Mahoney, celebrating with a promise to drop the belts on Vince McMahon's desk. However, Tommy Dreamer came out at the end of the night and wound up in an impromptu match, with Raven (who had called Eric Bischoff's bluff on a promise to allow any WCW star who was unhappy to leave the company) making an unannounced run-in to land a DDT and create an unlikely championship pairing.

Having lost their leading tag team, ECW was also about to lose its heavyweight champion to the WWF. After Taz began negotiations to jump to the WWF at the end of the year, ECW offered him a three year guaranteed contract for $380,000 a year, almost double what anyone else in the company was making. However, although he started being paid at the new rate, Taz never signed the deal. With the dangers of the deal setting an untenable precedent for salary demands, and ECW's financial status making any guarantee somewhat less than a true certainty, it was arguably better for both parties when Taz instead agreed to a $250,000 WWF contract.

His departure came on ECW's biggest show to date, drawing

almost 6,000 fans and the company's first $200,000 gate. The Anarchy Rulz pay-per-view was the most well-received of the year, with Lance Storm beating Jerry Lynn, Credible upsetting Sabu, and Tajiri winning a three-way against Super Crazy and Little Guido in what would become an undercard staple of the next year. In the main event (which actually took place third from top, a Van Dam-Mahoney stunt show ending the evening), a scheduled Taz vs Masato Tanaka match turned into a surprise three-way with Mike Awesome. Taz was pinned by both opponents in two minutes, allowing him to have a classy send-off before Awesome won what effectively became a one-on-one match with Tanaka that put both men, and the title, in the spotlight rather than dwelling on the loss of Taz.

By this point, there was some minor but growing concern about the TNN show's performance. The original concept was to make it heavy on in-ring action to contrast with the soap opera style of WWF and WCW programming. However, the format didn't catch on immediately with viewers. The first few shows were built around the Van Dam-Lynn rivalry, with an original plan of Van Dam losing the TV title, but winning the heavyweight title from Taz, both switches being dropped when Taz appeared to be staying with the company and Heyman decided to make Van Dam's quest for the main title into a long term story. The second TNN match between Van Dam and Lynn was actually taped for the syndicated show (now rebranded *Hardcore TV*), but got such a strong reaction that Heyman persuaded TNN to air it, even though it was taped with low-budget production at the ECW Arena. But while the show's debut rating of 0.94 had been touted as starting point for long-term growth (TNN was selling advertising slots on the basis of an average 1.9 rating), the ratings were now falling with the show featuring the Philadelphia match down to 0.72, barely a tenth of the wrestling audience that had watched the head to head WCW and WWF shows the previous evening.

The focus of the show abruptly changed to shorter matches and more emphasis on female characters such as Dawn Marie, Miss Congeniality (later Lita), Tammy Sytch and Francine, all of whom were featured in regular catfights while scantily clad. One week's show was even built around an 'insider' interview with Sytch talking about her much-rumoured personal problems, which many critics saw as tacky and exploitative. (In hindsight the timing proved particularly unfortunate when she mysteriously passed out in the ECW Arena dressing room two weeks later; at the end of the year she, partner Chris Candido and Axl Rotten were all let go by the company.)

Although the ratings were back at around the 1.0 level, they hovered there consistently for the next five months, with the lack of growth exacerbating the irritation between ECW and TNN. It was TNN's parent company CBS that had set-up the deal, hoping to capitalise on the success of televised wrestling to provide a lead-in audience for the Roller Jam show which followed ECW; TNN officials were less enthusiastic about carrying wrestling. At one point the station ordered ECW to stop using wrestler promos, music videos, or background music while an announcer was speaking, though CBS later overruled them. TNN also rejected several segments such that on one week's show Heyman cancelled his original plans and simply aired two undercard matches from Anarchy Rulz plus the Sytch interview.

However, Heyman was not seen as blameless. His insistence on keeping control of all aspects of the product was becoming unworkable with two television shows to produce each week plus house shows to organise. The seat-of-the-pants booking was not translating well to the demands of producing network television, and house shows were beginning to show signs of losing priority. ECW events had always been based on competitive matches, but the need to save major bouts for television and six pay-per-views a year was starting to become apparent, particularly with Awesome's house show opponents including such unlikely title challengers as Little Guido and Simon Diamond. With signs that wrestlers were starting to struggle to balance the needs of an all-out style with concerns about injuries, it was a welcome relief when the company switched back to two shows a week from the start of the new year (though it wasn't such good news for the undercard wrestlers who were paid nightly).

Live event business during the TNN era was a mixed bag. Most of the shows in smaller venues were dropped, upping the average gate, and ECW made its debut in nine new states, as far afield as Tennessee, Kansas and Texas. But regular venues were in decline, and follow-up shows in the new cities did not fare as well (the most extreme case being Wichita, Kansas which fell from 2,350 to 750, again the result of poor advertising). While some shows were still pulling in impressive crowds, the break-even figure of 1,700 was only averaged for two months during the year, suggesting the national TV exposure failed to bring the necessary leap in business. There was, however, one moral victory in March 2000 when the company's average attendance beat that of the freefalling WCW.

Inside the ring, the product was back to its familiar pattern of competent effort-filled performances lacking any major creative innovation. The two most memorable angles from the turn of the year saw upstart mouthy heel Steve Corino invade the stage during a Limp Bizkit concert (held in the same complex as an ECW show), only to be seen off by a Balls Mahoney chairshot, earning mainstream publicity on MTV; and Awesome apparently knocking out the teeth of a female Spike Dudley fan (who was actually the company's lighting director Kari Bullock, who had lost her real teeth in a previous accident). The return of the Sandman received a tremendous ovation and appeared to spike business in the Philadelphia area, but the results of wear and tear meant the performances of he, Dreamer and Raven as lead babyfaces seemed to lack their past inspiration. The trio headlined November to Remember against Storm, Credible and newcomer Rhino, with Taz's final match (an unsuccessful challenge for Van Dam's TV title) and another Awesome-Tanaka match the other major attractions. The January Guilty as Charged pay-per-view had Awesome beating Spike, Credible and Storm over Raven and Dreamer (when Raven sacrificed himself to save Dreamer from a caneshot) and another Sabu-Van Dam bout. While the show impressed in the ring, overly-familiar aspects (a New Jack brawl, a combination of Lynn, Tajiri, Guido and Crazy, and undercard clusters which often bore little relation to the originally scheduled match) meant the shows were starting to come off as formulaic. Indeed, the most high-profile bouts of the time were on television, with Awesome and Tanaka exchanging the heavyweight title in Nashville and White Plains.

Having lost $3.5 million dollars in 1999, funding was still heavily stretched. On 31 January, ECW took another loan from Acclaim, for $175,000, to be repaid ten days later. They also took a separate loan from Acclaim on the same day, this one for $350,000 to be repaid at the end of June. Neither loan was repaid at any point, which later raised even more questions about whether they constituted straightforward lending or were instead funding to keep the company in business.

The main on-screen storyline of the period was, on the face of it, extremely odd. As far back as Anarchy Rulz, new colour commentator Don 'Cyrus' Callis had positioned himself as a mysterious evil authority figure who claimed to have the power to get Styles into trouble with management. By the first show of 2000, his character was more explicitly explained: he was a representative of "the Network". In a thinly veiled dig at TNN's Nashville roots, he warned the now-babyface Joel Gertner not to make derogatory comments about country music, *Dallas*, *Dukes of Hazzard*, in-breeding, Garth Brooks or "*RollllllllllllerJam!*". Yes, a television show based on roller skating races was more disliked by the ECW audience than any wrestler. Rhino, Corino, Jack Victory and Tajiri all joined Cyrus as the Network's henchmen, and real-life problems were blamed on the group. When Rob Van Dam broke his leg, the Network ordered the TV title vacant, ending a 20 month reign, claiming that the station needed an active champion to drive up ratings. Even the temporary loss of Super Crazy over work visa problems was blamed on Network interference.

The root of the angle lay just eleven days after ECW's TNN debut when parent company CBS merged with Viacom (owners of stations such as MTV and numerous media groups). Soon after the merger's announcement, the WWF began negotiating to move its shows from USA (their home for the past 16 years) to the new network, with a deal involving *RAW* heading to TNN; *Smackdown* already aired on UPN, which was partially owned by Viacom. USA made counter-offers in December and January, but WWF turned them down and officially gave notice of their departure from the station on 1 March 2000. USA responded by starting legal action to stop the move, citing a clause in their contract which gave them the right to match any offer from a rival network. This was the first public announcement of the planned move, though it is clear that, whether through specific conversations with Vince McMahon, or simply the wrestling grapevine, Heyman was aware of the plans well before this date and made the moves to cast TNN as the villainous party to his audience.

The on-screen storyline appeared to be reflecting genuine discontent with TNN's handling of the show, which included the inexplicable decision to run commercials for the show *while it was airing*, with witless officials explaining that research showed this was the best time to reach the target audience. It wasn't until February that substantial television advertising began, with the "ThrillZone Friday" package of ECW and *RollerJam* being trailed during *RAW* and *Nitro*. But there was also tension on TNN's part: they cut the audio on a Joel Gertner promo and digitised his mouth to prevent lipreading, apparently feeling the phrase "I'd beat the women off of me, but that would be a waste, because you know they like the size of my stick, and you know they love the taste!" was unsuitable for broadcast at 8pm.

Tension was also on display in the run-up to the March pay-per-view, Living Dangerously. A week before the show Sabu, who had signed a deal with WCW despite being under contract, arrived at the ECW Arena and received a typed script calling for him to lose to Super Crazy during a three-way match with CW Anderson. This was the first time Heyman had ever specifically written out a script (as opposed to jotting plans on a napkin), and for good reason: after Sabu, as predicted, refused to lose the match and walked out, Heyman had written evidence that he had breached his contract.

For the pay-per-view itself, no matches were announced on TV until two days before the show. Heyman had by now concluded the paying audience was going to be roughly the same no matter what he advertised, and the figures bore out his theory: once the pay-per-views were carried by all the major distributors, the difference between the best and worst performing shows appears to have been 10,000 viewers or so. (The buyrates and house show attendance figures reported during this period are clearly unreliable; were all figures reported for 1999 accurate, ECW's income would have been around two-thirds higher than the legitimate amount that was later revealed in court filings.) With a main event of Super Crazy over Rhino for the vacant TV title, and Awesome defending the ECW title in the third match of the show against Kid Kash, it appeared blockbuster line-ups were no longer guaranteed. The ramshackle feel was only strengthened by the longest match going just 10 minutes, and the show ending around half an hour earlier than the timeslot would have allowed.

But one moment was memorable for all the wrong reasons. New Jack and the 400lbs Vic Grimes climbed to a scaffold thirteen feet above the ground. This was hardly out of the ordinary, except that neither man had given any thought to what they would do there. Climbing down was not an option thanks to the expectations previous falls and dives had created, but there wasn't enough room to do anything resembling a wrestling hold or throw. Instead they took hold of one another and jumped together, with New Jack crashing through a table and hitting the concrete, and Grimes landing directly on New Jack's head a split-second later. With blood pouring from his skull, many on hand briefly thought New Jack was dead. In the event he escaped with concussion, heavy bruising and a cracked elbow, but the permanent effects included hampered vision in one eye and problems with long-term memory.

The bad news continued when Awesome failed to appear at two house shows, giving false stories about travel problems. It soon became apparent he had in fact jumped to WCW for a contract worth a million dollars over four years, with the immediate concern being that he would throw the belt into a garbage can on the next edition of *Nitro* in a replication of a 1995 incident when then WWF Women's champion Alundra Blayze (Madusa) joined the promotion. Attempts to get a restraining order against Awesome and WCW did not produce anything in time for the show but, with the threat of legal action, WCW and ECW came to an agreement. Awesome would get a release from his contract in return for a WCW payment to ECW described as being "in the low six figures", with Awesome agreeing that for his *Nitro* debut he would appear in street clothes and without the title belt, and would wrestle in Indianapolis three days later to drop the ECW title. The deal also said WCW would introduce him as ECW champion, plug the Indianapolis match, and plug the TNN show, none of which they did. Heyman immediately began asking as many ECW stars as possible to sign binding contracts to prevent a similar situation.

At the Indianapolis show, Awesome arrived with WCW

security head Doug Dillinger and, rather than go to the dressing room, walked through the crowd, dropped the title in just over a minute, and left through the crowd. But the most bizarre thing about the match was his opponent: Taz. Thanks to a temporary talent loan, a WWF wrestler had just beaten a WCW wrestler for the ECW title.

What seemed a clever way to surprise fans soon looked questionable when Taz followed a string of low-profile losses over the weekend on WWF shows with a defeat by WWF champion Hunter Hearst Helmsley on *Smackdown* after backfired interference by Dreamer. It appeared the WWF's assistance had come at a price. The swerves continued the following Saturday at ECW Arena where, as expected, Taz dropped the belt to Dreamer, only for Justin Credible to win the belt in an impromptu challenge just minutes later. Credible had been pencilled in for the title reign for a long time, but the belt had now changed hands six times in seven months, compared to two and half years elapsing during the previous six reigns. Unlikely as it might seem today for a devalued championship to affect business, the decline in ECW TV ratings began with the show on which Awesome lost the title, and never returned to that level.

With the loan of Taz, following on from ECW using WWF clips during the Sytch interview, plus talks of Shawn Michaels making a non-wrestling guest appearance at Guilty as Charged and WWF developmental wrestlers Mic Tierney and Glen Kulkna being assigned to ECW (neither proposal coming to fruition), speculation again began about the relationship between the two companies. Heyman had admitted WWF had offered to loan him money the previous summer, but said he'd turned it down for fear of losing his independence. In October of 1999 he again denied any financial link between the two companies. In April 2000 he told the *Pro Wrestling Torch* that "I never borrowed one penny from the WWF or Vince McMahon in any way, shape or form." Though WWF did go on to lend money to ECW, at this point Heyman was telling the truth.

At this time ECW also turned down an offer by a group of former WCW executives, backed by a venture capital bank, to buy a 50.1% share in the company while giving Heyman a lifetime contract with full creative control. The group's head, Jay Hassman, later took a marketing role with Jeff Jarrett's NWA-TNA group which ended with his being fired over undisclosed links with the WWF.

Relations with TNN remained strained, particularly after TNN brought up the idea of moving the show to Tuesday and Heyman responded by suggesting the station was treating ECW "like a leprosy afflicted crack whore". On-screen rebellion reigned from the subtle (while supposedly speaking in tongues, Jim 'Sinister Minister' Mitchell slipped in the words "dildos in vaginas, fizuck Russo") to the blatant (returning from a break, Heyman welcomed viewers by saying he too was sick of commercials, but TNN needed the money to pay a hundred million dollars to the WWF).

One week's show featured a Heyman promo with the audio removed and an on-screen crawler reading "Please ignore this gentleman's temper tantrum. Could it be he's been thrown through too many tables? TNN harbors no ill feelings towards ECW. TNN supports ECW wrestling and all of its redeeming qualities." Later in the same show a Gertner promo aired with his voice removed, and a TNN graphic claiming technical difficulties, though the segment ended with Heyman's head popping into shot and the words "Are you ready to throw me off the air yet, pigfuckers?" were audible. Crowd noise played during the Gertner promo, suggesting the tape was produced by ECW in a way that would allow the 'censorship'. TNN publicist David Schwartz refused to comment on whether the dispute was being exaggerated on screen, telling the *Torch* "That's the beauty of wrestling. Even the people who follow it don't know what is real and what isn't." Either way, ECW was keeping its options open, sending TNN formal notice that the network had breached their contract and threatening legal action; with the costs of such a case likely prohibitive, it seems the main aim was to start the wheels in motion to get out of the TNN contract in case the WWF ended up staying on USA.

Cashflow was again becoming a problem. In early June, the pay of salaried wrestlers started falling behind, with most people owed two weeks' money, raising the tension backstage (which wasn't helped when Sandman went out for a match even drunker than usual, exposed himself to the crowd, then wound up fighting in a lavatory stall with Jack Victory). Wrestlers who began checking the details of their contracts found that if they wanted to file a claim for non-payment they would have to do so in the federal court, and ECW would have 30 days to make up the money. Cutbacks were becoming visible, with only the bare minimum necessary talent roster flown to TV tapings, and publicity for house shows now consisting mainly of handing out flyers, with little paid advertising.

And then came the news to which the company had become resigned. On 27 June, a court ruled that WWF could indeed move to TNN; although USA was able to match the financial details of the Viacom offer, they could not duplicate the associated benefits, such as a book deal with the Viacom-owned Simon & Schuster.

Two days later, TNN issued a public statement saying "ECW has failed to meet some of the criteria of the agreement, including ratings performance targets." ECW argued that meeting the ratings was impossible because of a lack of promotion by the network, but the conditions of their contract made this irrelevant. Effective 22 September, ECW's main TV show was cancelled.

22: Decline

"I know that when [Heyman] signs the [TV] deal, the first thing that'll happen is that we'll all get checks covering the back pay." (Steve Corino, Pro Wrestling Torch, *12 December 2000)*

Despite the loss of its main television show, ECW still had pay-per-views to produce. After a largely uneventful Hardcore Heaven in May (main-evented by Justin Credible beating his WCW-bound partner Lance Storm, with another Rob Van Dam-Jerry Lynn match as support), Heatwave in July proved more newsworthy, though not for the intended reasons. The show, held at the Olympic Auditorium in Los Angeles, was the promotion's West coast debut, and they earned the unwelcome attention of the California-based Xtreme Pro Wrestling group.

However, this wasn't just a case of territorial squabbling: XPW and ECW had an 18-month history. XPW's owner, a hardcore pornographer named Robert Zicari (professional name Rob Black), had become socially acquainted with Bubba Ray and Big Dick Dudley and visited ECW events. The relationship grew to the point that Black, girlfriend Janet Romano (who performed in movies as Lizzie Borden) and hardcore porn legend Tom Byron appeared at a Queens show in December 1998 in the corner of Little Guido. Around the same time, Bubba, Big Dick and Tommy Dreamer appeared in one of Black's productions, the self-explanatory *Whack Attack 4*, though the appearance was purely as onlookers rather than active participants!

Stories soon began floating around the adult movie industry that Black and ECW would be working together to cross-promote to their mutual target audience of young males. Speaking at the time, Black said there was a possibility of him promoting ECW videos and live events in Brazil, while there was also talk of ECW getting access to Black's superior television production equipment. One rumour even had it that Byron would appear on ECW television in a spoof of WWF character Val Venis (himself a spoof of porn actors). However, any potential relationship broke down, apparently due in part to a previous disagreement between Black and ECW's Steve Karel (who had been involved in soft porn production), but also because any involvement with Black's firm would likely threaten the TNN deal. Black went on to form XPW and started using former ECW talent such as Big Dick and the Pitbulls, with ECW looking into legal action over trademark infringement and contract interference.

Black bought six front row tickets to the Heatwave pay-per-view and sent XPW wrestlers to the show. Security kept a close eye on them, but there were no problems until the Dreamer-Credible main event. XPW valet Krysti Myst removed her top (revealing a leather bra), which raised the ire of Credible's valet Francine who was planning to do the same as part of the match, probably to distract the referee. The pair got into a shoving match which prompted security staff to get involved. As the cameras cut away, ECW wrestlers came from the locker room then moved outside the building where a mass brawl broke out, with ECW having about a three-to-one advantage (even Paul Heyman got involved) and the XPW crew escaping in a limo. Both sides talked of taking legal action but, most likely because neither party would come off as blameless, the dispute never made it to court.

Despite such interruptions, Heyman's main focus was on securing a new television deal, with negotiations not helped by the fact there was still no confirmed date for their departure from TNN as USA was appealing against the court decision about the WWF move. To make things even more complicated, ECW's main hope seemed to be a slot on USA, with talk of airing at 6pm on Saturdays, the traditional slot for WCW's main show throughout the seventies and eighties. Heyman was proposing a reality-based show to be produced by the team behind MTV's *The Real World*, apparently to mix in-ring action with documentary-style backstage footage. Heyman was now spending so much time on keeping ECW on air that he missed production of one week's TV, the first time he had not been involved in an episode in seven years.

Despite the problems, ECW still had some bright spots. Its Manhattan debut, two nights in the Hammerstein Ballroom (part of the Manhattan Center complex which was the original home of *RAW*), drew 2,500 sellouts each night for a combined gate of nearly

$250,000 including merchandise sales. The first night had a tournament for the vacant tag titles, won by Mikey Whipwreck and Yoshihiro Tajiri. The second night, rated by many as the best ECW non-PPV show in years, included the new FBI of Little Guido and Tony Mamaluke winning the tag titles, Credible successfully defending against Steve Corino in a match filled with convincing near-falls, and Kid Kash winning the TV title from Rhino. The strangest moment came when Cyrus 'officially' announced the cancellation of the TNN show, prompting perhaps the first "USA! USA!" chant in wrestling history to have nothing to do with patriotism. The shows even got extensive coverage in the city's *Daily News*.

Other live event debuts were also successful, with shows in Dallas and Houston getting crowds of 2,000 and 2,300 respectively, and Huntington, West Virginia getting 3,000 for a TV taping. The company's first overseas show, in Ontario, drew a 5,000 sellout. But signs elsewhere were worrying, with the crowd in the traditionally strong Buffalo market at 2,000, little more than half the usual level. Heyman cancelled shows in Iowa and Nebraska, realising there was little if any prospect of them breaking even, which meant further problems for the undercard wrestlers who were paid by the match. Those on salaries were also facing problems: another missed set of payoffs was blamed on delay in getting the money from the Ontario show back across the border but, whatever the reason, many performers were now a month behind on pay.

With finances being as tight as ever Heyman finally accepted Vince McMahon's offer of financial assistance, taking money at some point between July and December. ECW wound up owing the WWF $587,500 for "Work, labor and services/and or goods sold and delivered", a generic catch-all phrase that appears in this case to have been a simple loan. McMahon has said the money was simply to help keep the company afloat and provide a place for talent to develop, though there is also the possibility he was lining himself up as a significant creditor in any bankruptcy, giving him a strong claim to getting his hands on the company's wrestling-related assets at a knock-down price.

After a well-received Anarchy Rulz pay-per-view, headlined by Jerry Lynn capturing the ECW title from Credible, and a somewhat less athletic showdown between Joel Gertner and Cyrus, two events in the space of a week dealt what was effectively the death sentence to the company. Heyman had met with TNN to discuss the future of the show, which was still airing as McMahon had waived his exclusivity clause until the end of the year. However, the two sides could not come to an agreement; indeed, the meetings led to disputes over whether or not ECW owed TNN a portion of its pay-per-view receipts from the past year. On 11 October TNN announced the show was cancelled immediately, meaning viewers were left hanging. Six days later, a spokesman for USA Network told the *Pro Wrestling Torch* that "we are not negotiating with ECW". Whether a final decision had been taken at this point is disputable, but it was soon clear that USA would not be carrying ECW. While Heyman had been negotiating with the company's president Stephen Chao, USA chairman Barry Diller came down against the deal, partly because he was not prepared for the network to either pay a programming fee or buy into the company; notwithstanding ECW's financial problems, Heyman could not even produce organised and accurate financial records for potential investors. Diller was also wary of negative publicity from action groups such as the Parents Television Council, which had lobbied against the WWF's more controversial storylines, and had now shown signs of turning its attention to ECW. And Diller argued that wrestling's traditionally successful viewing figures were not as beneficial as they seemed because the wrestling audience tended not stick with the channel for whichever show followed wrestling.

With the USA deal dead, Heyman began a series of cross-country trips to negotiate with TV executives from stations such as FX and ESPN2, but there seemed no way of finding a deal that would not only give the company the necessary exposure to maintain its audience but would do so in a way that was financially viable. Fox Sports Net (which later carried NWA-TNA) offered a daily weekday afternoon slot, but this was hardly conducive to ECW's product or capabilities. Clips of ECW shows appeared on *Farmclub.com*, a music show produced by Universal (the world's largest record label) and aired on USA Network, with videos by Universal artists appearing on ECW pay-per-views. Precise details of the deal were kept quiet, but it somehow wound up with ECW owing $300,000.

With no prospect of national TV, ECW was now simply trying to survive from week-to-week. For a weekend's shows in Virginia, no wrestlers were flown in, with only those who could drive to the towns appearing on the shows. The following weekend's shows in New Jersey and Allentown, Pennsylvania were cancelled. After the November to Remember pay-per-view (headlined by Corino winning the world title in a 'double jeopardy' match also featuring Lynn, Sandman and Credible, with the main excitement coming backstage when Jim Mitchell mistakenly blew part of his finger off while experimenting with plans to throw a fireball), only two house shows took place before a series of four cancellations in the Mid-West. After another pay-per-view, Massacre on 34th Street in Manhattan (headlined by Corino beating Credible and Lynn in a three-way), cancelled shows in Texas meant there were just five events left on the ECW calendar. At the end of the year, despite the TNN exposure, revenue was down almost a third on 1999.

By this point, another payoff to salaried wrestlers was delayed, putting them six weeks behind at one stage. Rob Van Dam had filed a claim for breach of contract and had not appeared on a show since October. Others were in a worse position: Credible, whose wife had just given birth without medical insurance, said he couldn't risk filing a claim in case it led to his pay being cut off completely during the time the company had to respond to such a claim. Heyman was now beginning to talk of allowing some of the major names to begin negotiating elsewhere, running a bare-bones company with just a handful of contracted talent, and shoring up the card with night-by-night workers. He admitted that the existing structure of the company was not financially viable, with television too expensive to maintain, but necessary if the company was to draw enough to survive, particularly when it came to merchandise sales. There was even talk that he'd be prepared to sell the company, but his demands that all existing debts be cleared and talent contracts honoured made it unlikely anyone would buy.

After a show in Queens organised by the on-loan Dudleys (with an unannounced appearance by Taz) which was openly promoted to raise money, with tickets at $40 and $60, the last company show at the ECW Arena took place on 23 December, with

Corino vs Credible vs Sandman the final match, though there was no formal acknowledgement or acceptance that this was a farewell to the venue. By the time of the Guilty as Charged pay-per-view on 7 January the company had dropped its television deal with MSG and, having failed to send a new television episode that week to the Philadelphia station, appeared to have given up producing its syndicated show. After the event, highlighted by Sandman winning the ECW title but dropping it immediately to Rhino, and Van Dam making a one-night return to beat Lynn one more time, the usual promo tapings did not take place, apparently confirming the end of television.

As it happened, Heyman sent cameras to the next show, in Poplar Bluff, Missouri, an event sold for a flat fee to a local promoter. However, many of the key performers were missing in an attempt to keep costs down, with Lynn, Corino, Kash, Whipwreck and Balls Mahoney among the notable absentees. The following night's show in Pine Bluff, Missouri ended with Sandman beating Credible followed by an in-ring celebration by the entire roster to mark what was accurately suspected to be the final ECW show. The attempts to keep good spirits were not helped by the absence of payoffs for salaried wrestlers, putting them nine weeks behind.

As rumours of potential buyers became ludicrous at both ends of the scale, from Mexican promoter Antonio Pena supposedly offering just $200,000, to a hastily-denied story of the company being offered to Billy Corgan of the Smashing Pumpkins band for $10 million, the roster began seriously looking elsewhere. The WWF signed Credible to a contract and opened negotiations with Rhino and Tajiri, promising to keep the talks quiet to avoid giving the impression ECW was a sinking ship. Corino, Dawn Marie and Simon Diamond went to a *Nitro* taping looking for work. Nobody from ECW went to the National Association of Television Production Executives (NATPE) convention in February, ending any hope the company might still be looking at relaunching its syndicated show.

And then on 3 March, after announcer Jerry Lawler quit the WWF in protest at the firing of his girlfriend Stacey 'Miss Kitty' Carter, Paul Heyman debuted as the new colour commentator on *RAW*, having recently signed a five-year WWF contract. Noting that he wore an ECW baseball cap, the most delusional fanatics tried to convince themselves it was just a publicity ploy that would lead to the revitalisation of the company.

But ECW was done.

23: Aftermath

"As an accountant, not knowing why ECW folded is a frustrating concept. I'd like to be able to finish the puzzle. As an ECW fan, though, it just doesn't seem to matter." (Bob Kapur, SLAM! Wrestling website, April 2001)

On 4 April 2001, HHG Inc, the parent company of ECW, filed for bankruptcy. It listed total liabilities (money owed by ECW) of $8,881,435 and total assets (ECW's property and money owed to ECW) of $1,385,500, putting it just short of seven and a half million dollars in debt.

The major creditors (people and organisations owed money) were:

* **Richard S Heyman** (Paul's father) ($3,575,429)
* **Annodeus** (Parent company of Acclaim) ($1,000,000)
* **World Wrestling Federation Entertainment** ($587,500)
* **Farm Club Online** ($300,000)
* **The Original San Francisco Toymakers** ($250,000)
* **MSG Network** ($244,000)
* **American Cable Productions** (Parent company of the America One television network) ($243,000)
* **Sulamita Heyman** (Relationship unknown, though Sulamita was Richard Heyman's middle name) ($226,500)
* **Eugene R Boffa, Jr** (Lawyer) ($188,000)
* **Eugene J Ciarkowski** (ECW's Chief Financial Officer) ($183,000)
* **In Demand** ($150,000)
* **Robert 'Rob Van Dam' Szatkowski** ($150,000)
* **Hoffinger, Friedland, Dobrish & Stern** (Lawyers) ($140,000)
* **Paul Heyman** ($128,000) (Back pay; as an officer of the company, bankruptcy laws meant he would get $4,300 of this at

most)

       * **Advanced Transportation Services** ($125,140)
       * **Thomas 'Tommy Dreamer' Laughlin** ($100,000)
       * **TNN Cable** ("Unknown")

Other ECW performers owed money (sums listed where available) were: **Angel** Medina ($500); **Anthony DeVito** ($500); Brian **'Julio Deniro'** Woe ($300); Carlene **'Jazz'** Moore ($1,000); Charles John **'Tony Mamaluke'** Spencer ($600); **Chris Hamrick** ($300); Christopher **'CW Anderson'** Wright ($500); **Dan 'Doring'** Morrison ($2,100); **Dawn Marie** Psalpis ($9,000); Don **'Cyrus'** Callis ($12,000); Donna **'Elektra'** Adamo; **Francine** Fournier ($47,275); Francisco **'Super Crazy'** Islas ($5,000); James **'Sandman'** Fullington; James **'Little Guido'** Maritato; James **'Sinister Minister'** Mitchell; **James Molineaux**; Jason **'EZ Money'** Broyles ($300); Jerome **'New Jack'** Young ($5,000); **Jerry Lynn**; **John Finnegan**; John **'Mikey Whipwreck'** Watson ($12,000); Jon **'Balls Mahoney'** Rechner ($4,000); Joseph **'Joey Styles'** Bonsignore ($50,480); Joseph **'Johnny Swinger'** Dorgan; Ken **'Jack Victory'** Reininghaus; Lou **'Sign Guy Dudley/Lou E Dangerously'** D'Angeli; Matt **'Spike Dudley'** Hyson; Michael **'Nova'** Bucci ($4,000); Michael **'Roadkill'** DePaoli ($21,250); **Michael Kehner** (referee); Patrick **'Simon Diamond'** Kenney; Peter **'Justin Credible'** Polaco ($7,990); **Scott 'Anton'** Antol; **Steve Corino** ("None"); Terry **'Sabu'** Brunk ("None"); Terry **'Rhino'** Gerin ($50,000); **Thomas Marquez** ($500); Troy **'Shane Douglas'** Martin ($48,000); William **'Chilly Willy'** Jones ($500); **William Alfonso**; William **'Wild Bill'** Wiles; **Yoshihiro Tajiri** ($5,000). Several wrestlers disputed the amounts, most likely because they were expecting pay-per-view payoffs which the company considered optional bonuses. Those for whom no sum was listed were not included in the total figure for ECW's debts.

ECW employees and associates listed included Steve Karel ($50,000), Gabe Sapolsky ($1,400), Debra Beaumont, local promoter Gregory Bagarozy ($20,577), event promoter Dan Kowal, pay-per-view director Michael Vettor and Atlas Protection (ECW's security firm). Other creditors included nine different legal firms, and various production companies (owed just over $250,000 between them).

The filing showed that as well as paying for TV on MSG Network and America One, ECW owed money to stations in Chicago ($60,000 to Weigel Broadcasting Company), Philadelphia, Pittsburgh, Buffalo, Central Illinois, Virginia and Alabama. They also owed money, most likely for advertising, to radio stations in Nebraska, Iowa, Massachusetts, Ohio and Georgia. And the creditors included seven arenas, one of which had last been run by ECW in April 2000.

The full list of creditors included more than 100 other individuals and businesses, including several fans who were members of the 'Club ECW' system for buying advance tickets, J-Mar (producers of championship belts), various tax authorities ($35,000 total), and PTN Media, a company which developed celebrity-branded products and was responsible for the WCW *Nitro* cologne; it seems unlikely a similar product was being developed for ECW! There were also 13 outstanding lawsuits listed with a potential liability.

The list of ECW's assets included estimated money owed from In Demand ($800,000), Acclaim ($10,000) and Original San Francisco Toymakers ($10,000). The company's videotape library was listed with an estimated value of $500,000. The only other assets listed were a truck used for carrying merchandise (valued at $19,500, but bought on credit with $14,455 left to pay), $4,000 in merchandise and $2,000 in a Jersey City bank account.

The bankruptcy rules meant that priority went to those with a 'secured asset', that is claim to a specific item or part of the business, plus the tax authorities. Other than Ford having priority on the truck, Annodeus argued that it had a secured claim for $1,400,000 (disputing the listed amount) which would take all the remaining assets. However, on 16 April the WWF offered $737,500 for the 'non-cash assets' of the company. This offer involved WWF wiping clean the debt it was owed by ECW, plus paying $150,000 for the tape library. (The court turned down this offer.)

Although the original bankruptcy filing had been of the 'Chapter 11' type, in which the company only seeks temporary protection for creditors, while attempting to get its finances in order and continue doing business, it was clear this was not a serious prospect. When Heyman failed to appear at a court hearing, the court ordered the case to be reclassified as a 'Chapter 7' type, in which the company is closed and the court makes its best efforts to collect assets and settle debts. By this point it was clear the case would likely involve collecting the money from In Demand and then deciding how the assets were divided between Annodeus (who had the most money due to them) and the WWF (who were the only creditor with any real use for the wrestling-related assets).

Heyman himself filed for personal bankruptcy on 22 June, listing debts of $2.7 million, covering some but not all of the debts in the company filing, apparently those in which he signed the relevant agreements as an individual as well as an officer of the company. His filing listed his salary with the WWF as $4,000 a month, which appeared to be far below the amount the WWF would pay somebody who was both a writer and television announcer. One theory has it that Heyman was working at a lower salary as a way of paying back the loans from the WWF, though if this was a formal arrangement it would have had to be registered with the bankruptcy court. There has been at least one suggestion that the salary was set to get around new bankruptcy laws under which people earning a certain figure would have repay some of their debts, but the figures involved do not bear this out. Heyman's only listed assets were the $128,000 he was owed in back pay (which he would not be getting) and $500 in clothing. What personal property he owned, other than that which was exempt from being taken by the courts, would clearly cover only a minute fraction of his debts, so his was declared a 'no asset' case, and eventually discharged and closed on 18 March 2002.

Shortly before ECW's bankruptcy filing, WWF had bought the assets of World Championship Wrestling and begun work to relaunch WCW as a wrestling brand under the storyline ownership of Shane McMahon. However, a combination of ego-driven booking errors and the negative stigma of WCW among WWF fans had meant the idea was not catching on. On the 9 July *RAW*, the WWF unveiled its latest angle, decided on just three days earlier. During a Kane & Chris Jericho vs Lance Storm and Mike Awesome match, Tommy Dreamer, Tazz, Raven, Justin Credible and new signing Rob Van

Dam came to ringside and attacked Kane & Jericho, with Paul Heyman announcing it as an ECW reunion. The WWF and 'WCW' wrestlers put their differences aside for a match later in the evening against the newly formed ECW group, only for the WCW wrestlers to immediately turn against the WWF. The show went off the air with the claim that Heyman had sold ECW to Stephanie McMahon, and that she and Shane were now united against father Vince's WWF.

The bankruptcy court was unimpressed, ordering such claims be stopped. WWF lawyers came up with the imaginative argument that, by not listing any trademarks as assets in the bankruptcy filing, Heyman/HHG Inc had abandoned any claim to the ECW name, and it was therefore free for anyone to use. (The failure to list the trademarks was at best a tremendous oversight, and at worst more cynical conclusions have been drawn.) To avoid legal action on either side, which would have been particularly costly as the WWF was producing an 'inter-promotional' pay-per-view on 22 July, bankruptcy trustee Barbara Balaber-Strauss came to an agreement by which the WWF would pay $50,000 for the use of the trademarks until the end of the month, which would also serve as a non-refundable deposit towards any future purchase of the trademarks. On the same day, the WWF filed an offer of $250,000 for the trademarks and the tape library.

WWF was under the impression that if nobody else bid more than this $250,000, they would automatically be allowed to buy the trademarks and tape library at that price. However, on 26 July, Annodeus filed a motion arguing that its contract with the company made it a priority creditor. Annodeus also said that they were owed $1,525,000 in total which, being more than ECW's total assets, meant they should get everything. The WWF and Heyman disputed this, saying the Annodeus figure did not take account of the royalties they owed ECW on the video game (which grossed $17 million in its first year) and that the money was funding to keep the company alive to protect the licence deal, rather than being a loan. The court put any settlements on hold while it looked over what passed for financial records in ECW; in the meantime WWF stopped using the name so heavily on television, referring to the WCW/ECW group simply as 'The Alliance'.

Whether through the complexity of ECW's finances, or the

traditionally slow pace of the legal system, it took until July of 2002 before the bankruptcy trustee came up with a proposal. (By this point, the storyline 'Alliance' had been defeated by the WWF, with a match stipulation meaning Stephanie McMahon's on-screen 'ECW' was finished.) In short, the trustee's plan would bring together the money owed by In Demand and royalties paid by Pioneer Entertainment, which distributed ECW DVDs in North America but had been missed off the original list of assets. From this, $375,000 would be earmarked for legal fees and settling ECW's tax bills, with the remaining money, tape library and trademarks going to Annodeus. The WWF (now renamed WWE) immediately objected and argued that, taking into account royalty payments and the technicalities of why Annodeus gave money to ECW, they were only automatically entitled to $600,000. Unfortunately this argument was based on the idea that nobody would lend money to the badly struggling ECW without taking some form of ownership or other involvement; the trustee pointed out that the WWF had done just that itself.

The objection meant the case dragged back until February 2003, when the trustee produced a new deal. ECW's wrestling-related assets (the trademarks and the rights to the video library) would be auctioned with a minimum bid of $1,280,000. Annodeus would get $2,000,000, paid for by the minimum bid and the money from In Demand. If the auction raised more than the minimum bid, the excess would be shared out among all creditors in proportion to the money they were owed.

With no other bidders, WWE successfully made the minimum bid. Including the $50,000 from 2001, which was no longer considered a deposit, and some legal loose ends that accompanied the sale, the company paid a total of $1,496,808.05 (though with associated costs, WWE budgeted the long-term expense of the deal at $3 million). Aside from Annodeus, no other creditors received any of the money they were owed.

As of 17 June 2003, the legacy of ECW belonged to Vince McMahon.

24: Resurrection

"This has been a night of genuine emotion." (Mick Foley, One Night Stand)

A curious thing happened after ECW and WCW stopped promoting in the spring of 2001 and were buried in storyline fashion in November. WCW, which had several years drawing more than a hundred million dollars, was all but forgotten, other than footage being used on WWE DVDs and its *24/7* video-on-demand service. Perhaps it was the natural result of a corporate giant with hundreds of employees going out of business. Perhaps it was the constant humiliation of the brand on WWE television. Perhaps it was simply the way the last 27 months of the company's history had seen terrible creative work drive away millions of fans. Whatever the case, WCW was dead.

ECW wouldn't die. The chants remained a common occurrence on WWE television whenever a former ECW star wrestled, or even simply when somebody performed a spectacular stunt. Independent groups tried to fill the gap and become the next ECW, from the aforementioned Combat Zone Wrestling ("Cee-Zee-Dubya! Cee-Zee-Dubya!) to the Blue Meanie's Pro-Pain Pro Wrestling (otherwise known as 3PW or "Three-Pee-Dubya! Three-Pee-Dubya!"), both of whom ran shows at Viking Hall. Another group, Major League Wrestling, used former ECW production staff including Joey Styles on commentary, with the look and feel of the TV show bearing more than a passing resemblance to ECW's TNN show. Former ECW stars found themselves a marketable commodity, even in an industry suddenly flooded with redundant talent. But ECW was still just a chant and a memory.

Then, just as the home video of The Night The Line Was Crossed brought the promotion to the forefront of the underground wrestling scene, a WWE DVD brought ECW back from the dead. Unlike *The Monday Night War*, a disappointing and highly partisan look at the WWF-WCW rivalry, *The Rise And Fall Of ECW* proved to be a compelling three-hour documentary which, while far from 100% accurate, was a surprisingly honest account of the promotion's history. On its release in November 2004, it became virtually impossible to find on many shelves, selling out entirely on pre-orders. In its first week it sold more than 22,000 copies, and at one point it was just a few thousand copies away from being the biggest-selling DVD in WWE history. Within a couple of weeks of the DVD's release, Vince McMahon approved a proposal to run a pay-per-view under the ECW brand in 2005, an idea suggested by Rob Van Dam, though there have been rumours he was acting as a mouthpiece for Heyman. In a strange piece of timing, days after the approval McMahon ended Heyman's second reign as a WWE writer/booker and demoted him to a token consultant role.

Fears soon began growing that the show would be a watered-down WWE production, fuelled by reports that WWE creative head Stephanie McMahon was insisting Heyman have nothing to do with the show, and that only performers under contract to WWE be used. Thankfully for the show, Heyman was eventually given the lead creative role of the event, albeit with tight supervision, with permission to bring in outside wrestlers (though several key performers including Raven were unable to appear because of their work for NWA-TNA, now the closest thing WWE had to a competitor).

Originally the show, from the Hammerstein Ballroom, was set to be promoted with little or no build-up beyond television commercials and posters on the streets of New York. However, with just four weeks to go to the 12 June 'One Night Stand' show, McMahon either got cold feet or listened to the whisperings of the anti-Heyman faction. A live discussion on *RAW* brought together McMahon, Heyman and Eric Bischoff for the first time on screen, with Bischoff threatening to sabotage the pay-per-view. However, McMahon 'revealed' that not only was he funding the event, but it was an attempt to make back the money he had spent attempting to keep ECW alive only for Bischoff's predatory talent raids to kill the company. The latest example of winners writing history seemed to be about the best possible way to kill any momentum the ECW concept had heading into the show. When the decision was made to announce no matches on television (releasing the line-up only on the WWE website) and to build the show around a group of WWE heels led by

Bischoff and Kurt Angle buying tickets and promising to disrupt the event, even the most optimistic fan was wary of how the event would go down.

One Night Stand wasn't the only ECW-related event of the weekend. Two days earlier, Shane Douglas ran an event titled Hardcore Homecoming at the former ECW Arena. (With a double-header by independent promotions CZW and IWA Mid South in the same building on the Saturday, and a Ring Of Honor show in Manhattan on the Sunday afternoon, it was quite the weekend for wrestling fans in the Northeast.) As with a documentary produced by Douglas' colleague Jeremy Borash, *Forever Hardcore*, the WWE purchase of the trademarks produced the bizarre sight of an ECW tribute show with former ECW wrestlers in the old ECW Arena, in which the letters ECW were never mentioned. Despite heavily-increased ticket prices, the show sold out before a planned paid advertising campaign launched, with the $135,000 gate more than tripling the previous record for a show in the building. With Tod Gordon welcoming the fans, Joey Styles, Cyrus and Joel Gertner opening the show, and a raucous crowd (though there appeared to be a far higher female proportion than in the ECW days), it was just like old times. Except for one thing.

The building, now renamed the New Alhambra, was *clean*. The new owners had renovated the building, now also used for boxing events and concerts, with corporate advertising by Miller Lite, office space, and even an actual dressing room. There was an entrance rampway and a big screen. A certain charm was gone forever, though with the temperature topping a hundred degrees, it was still the sweatbox everyone remembered.

The show was particularly true to ECW tradition in that it was presented buffet-style with something for everyone. The traditional heat-based tag action of Mikey Whipwreck and Chris Chetti over Simon Diamond and CW Anderson came first, followed by Tracy Smothers (with JT Smith) beating the Blue Meanie in a comedy bout, Too Cold Scorpio over Kid Kash in a slow-building but ultimately high-flying match, and John Kronus and New Jack battling Axl and Ian Rotten in a bloodbath. This match was originally scheduled as a reunion with the Gangstas vs the Eliminators, but Saturn's neck injury and Mustafa's apparent disappearance from the face of the earth led to the change; the brawl was not announced as an official match because the Rottens were still sticking to their promise to never team again, six and a half years after losing the match with that stipulation.

Jerry Lynn beat Justin Credible in the best match of the weekend, while Raven beat Sandman thanks to the interference of Don E Allen (in a '49F'n8' shirt to mark his much maligned highest placing in the *PWI500* rankings) and Whipwreck. And in the main event Sabu beat Terry Funk (who turned down a spot on the WWF show, figuring that at 60 he couldn't work two shows in a weekend) and Douglas in a barbed wire match; though such bouts were now illegal in Pennsylvania, the commission's cut of the spectacular gate was apparently a pleasant enough surprise to help them reconsider the regulations.

The difference between Hardcore Homecoming and One Night Stand was that everyone involved and attending the former knew what to expect (namely a series of well-worked matches before a hot, nostalgic crowd). But the latter could so easily have been an artistic disaster that left a bad taste in the mouths of its core audience. Instead it was a true blowaway event. While no matches on the show were anywhere close to classics, the atmosphere and feel of the show was like few other pay-per-views. In a world of scripted, controlled, take-it-or-leave-it monopolised productions, it was quite simply... real.

The chants and cheers and passion of the crowd started strong and never let up. Unlike a WWE show where periods of silence during the undercard had become common, the show was two and a half hours of cathartic release, as frustration at the state of the industry in 2005, and nostalgia for the happier times of ECW came together in explosive fashion. With Styles on commentary (accompanied by Mick Foley), ECW-style camera-work, Heyman producing, Bob Artese as ring announcer, ECW referees and even a smaller ECW-sized ring, WWE fingerprints seemed to have been wiped clean. In place of extensive backstage skits and promos, the show featured several packages of classic clips from ECW history.

Lance Storm, accompanied by Dawn Marie in his retirement match, beat former partner (and first-match opponent) Chris Jericho thanks to interference by Jason and Justin Credible. Super Crazy beat Tajiri (with Whipwreck and Sinister Minister) and Guido (with Smothers, Smith, Tony Mamaluke and even Big Guido) in a three way dance highlighted by Crazy moonsaulting from a balcony. Both matches set the tone for the undercard: solid, but too short, disappointing on first viewing thanks to high expectations, but perfectly adequate given the crowd response. The following Rey Mysterio vs Psicosis match, however, did not go down well with the crowd, which expected a re-run of their 1995 bouts, and responded with hearty boos to Psicosis working without his mask, Psicosis using a lengthy headlock, and Mysterio hitting the 619 (a 'WWE move'). Yet in some way the reaction only heightened the nostalgia: the unpredictable but unambiguous crowd was as much a part of ECW as any match.

Kurt Angle, John Bradshaw Layfield and their *Smackdown* colleagues showed up and took their seats next and, at this point, the WWE participation started to make sense. None of the fans wanted to boo any of the former ECW talents on such a nostalgic occasion, but the 'invaders' provided a focal point for a negative reaction; for this night, it was promotions and concepts, rather than match opponents, which represented good and evil. The crowd had so much fun ripping into the WWE performers (particularly Angle and JBL who both cut promos) and cheering an adlibbed Rob Van Dam in-ring interview condemning the way he had been used for the past four years, that many spectators managed to overlook the fact they had each put up to $400 in Vince McMahon's pocket.

The promo ended with a Rhyno run-in and the trademark dimming of the lights leading to a surprise appearance by Sabu and an impromptu added match, which the latter won in a short and sweet affair which didn't expose either man. Then came the arrival of the *RAW* crew, ranging from the ultimate heel Eric Bischoff (who provoked genuine hatred as he passed through the crowd) to Maven (whose objection to ECW seemed somewhat spurious considering he first began training several months after the promotion's demise). Unfortunately the crowd's barracking of the WWE stars, particularly recently exposed adulterer Edge, took much of the attention away from a Chris Benoit vs Eddy Guerrero bout. That said, while competently worked, the match never stepped into high gear, with

Guerrero seeming to be too concerned about maintaining his current WWE heel character to get into the expected 'mat classic'.

After a skit with Bischoff refusing to give Gertner a job, Mike Awesome and Masato Tanaka, a pairing added a few days before the event, stole the show. The commentary, in which Styles viciously laid into Awesome's 2000 departure from ECW only heightened the impact of the bout as Styles slowly came around to praising his performance. Though hardly subtle (except in the sense that slightly crazy stunt preceded extremely crazy stunt), the collection of brutal chairshots, powerbombs through tables and insane dives produced a match that nobody viewing would ever forget, but nobody with any compassion would ever want to see again.

After Heyman addressed the crowd, concluding with the memorable insider line that the only reason JBL held the WWE title for nine months was "because Triple H didn't want to work Tuesdays", it was main event time. Following the entrances of the Dudley Boys and Tommy Dreamer came the moment that was not just the highlight of the night, but the perfect microcosm of what ECW stood for.

Although the WWE crew had appeared to enjoy the show more than the storyline would suggest (and Gene Snitsky enjoyed the feet of a waitress in a bizarre moment which would later be referred to in a *RAW* skit), their out-of-character reactions had so far remained off-camera. But now they could be clearly seen looking on with expressions that showed they were simply unable to conceive or understand what was happening.

An out-of-shape, unathletic, scarred, and clearly intoxicated 42-year-old made his way from the balcony through the fans to the ring, to the sounds of Metallica's most famous song. And 2,500 people sang the lyrics while treating the Sandman as not just a wrestling babyface with a momentary pop, but as a legitimate, beloved, worshipped superstar. The match they were about to see was a pre-determined show. The passion they displayed was total unscripted reality.

The tradition of Heyman booking to cover the limitations of his performers was on display, with eighteen ECW characters involved in what was billed as a straight tag match. To kick things off, Sandman and Dreamer acknowledged Anderson and Chetti in the front row, then poured beer over the ample chest of former valet Elektra. Before the match could get started, the bWo came out with their full entrance. A predictable brawl broke out, with Kid Kash making an aborted attempt to get involved, followed by Axl Rotten and Balls Mahoney taking out Meanie and Nova with stiff chairshots. With everyone in the aisle, Kash ran across the ring, springboarded off the prone referee to the top rope, and flip-dived into the melee, recreating a spot from the night he won the TV title in the same building. Once the match proper began, there was little pretence at exchanging holds, beyond a simultaneous pair of figure-fours by Sandman and Dreamer. After a cheese grater and a ladder led to all four men bleeding, Storm and Credible ran out, with Credible piledriving Sandman onto a ball of barbed wire. Francine ran out and low-blowed Dreamer, leading to Beulah making her first wrestling appearance in seven years for one more catfight, followed by a low blow to take out Storm, and then a pair of DDTs by her and now-husband Dreamer on the Dudleys. Then came Spike Dudley, in his original ECW gear, bringing lighter fluid to set a table alight, with Dreamer powerbombed through the flames for the pin.

For most shows, that would be plenty of action for a main event. But there was more to come. Trying to revive Dreamer, Sandman elected not to call for a medic or smelling salts, but instead frantically screamed for somebody to bring him a beer. None other than Steve Austin answered his call, setting up an in-ring party with all the ECW performers, followed by Austin taunting the WWE crew to get into the ring for the inevitable showdown. Although the scheduled highlight was the arrival of Taz to choke out Angle in revenge for an attack on the previous episode of *Smackdown*, the mass brawl would become better known for an incident in which JBL legitimately blindsided Blue Meanie (apparently over personal issues between the two stemming from Meanie's brief WWF run) and then got the upper hand in the ensuing genuine fistfight.

Once the WWE 'invaders' had, inevitably, been run from the ring, all that remained was for Eric Bischoff to taste a Dudley 3D, a Benoit diving headbutt and an Austin Stone Cold Stunner before the Dudleys threw him out of the building. The event, booked by

Heyman as the ultimate fantasy ECW show bringing together characters from throughout the company's history, ended with Styles proclaiming "ECW lives!" as Sandman and Austin shared a beer, with no clear answer as to which was giving the superstar rub to the other.

For a few days, it seemed One Night Stand might change the course of the business. Early soundings from both insider newsletters and, more tellingly, Canadian closed circuit broadcasts, suggested a huge buyrate, though rumours of 800,000 buyers had no substantial basis. Some people talked of regular ECW pay-per-views, house show tours, even a weekly TV slot. Others questioned whether the high impact style was practical on a regular schedule, or if the nostalgia feeling would soon be played out. Many argued that the event had served as the farewell ECW never had, and that no future event could be anything but a letdown after what was a truly perfect night.

It certainly seemed as if the questions were answered almost immediately. Save for the bWo appearing on *Smackdown* for a Meanie-Layfield match built off the internet discussion of their brawl, only for the trio to quickly find themselves demoted to bit-player afterthoughts, ECW was as good as forgotten. As far as WWE storylines went, the show never happened. In a stockholder conference to cover the publication of WWE annual report 18 days after the show, there was no mention of ECW. And the DVD release suggested the company had either learned nothing from the experience or chosen to ignore the passion behind the show, passing up the seemingly-obvious idea of a Heyman or Dreamer audio commentary in favour of the one-note gag of using a live recording of JBL's in-character ramblings during the show, effectively giving buyers the 'bonus' of hearing somebody they disliked (in most cases genuinely) disparaging the product they had purchased.

Then came the buyrate. Cable industry insiders had reported a figure of between 390,000 and 430,000 which would have been a tremendous success, and in virtually every case in the past, the WWE's initial prediction was higher than the industry's figure. Yet curiously the WWE listed the show at 268,000 buys, below the *RAW* show Vengeance two weeks later which the WWE figures had at 315,000 buys, despite cable industry estimates that the ECW show did better business. (The WWE estimate for One Night Stand was later revised to 310,000 without fanfare.) But ultimately it didn't matter whether or not WWE was massaging its figures to placate fragile egos. Whatever the true figure, One Night Stand was clearly at a certain business level that could be used to justify anything from a full-scale resurrection of the brand to a complete banishment to history, depending entirely on the beliefs of whomever made the case.

With Heyman's WWE contract set to expire at the end of 2005, it seems increasingly possible that ECW's final official moment has already occurred.

At around 10.45pm on Sunday 12 June 2005, Tommy Dreamer walked to the ring at the Hammerstein Ballroom, knelt down on the bloody, dirty, beer-stained canvas, broke down in tears, and kissed the ECW logo.

25 – The extreme reality

Extreme Championship Wrestling was arguably the first sizeable promotion in America to specifically appeal to an audience that knew they were seeing a performance. The ECW faithful, from the Philadelphia core to followers of the tape-trading scene and online discussion, to the post-kayfabe national audience, understood that they were not watching a genuine contest. Indeed, the product was often delivered with a knowing wink towards off-screen antics.

Yet it never made any difference. ECW fans were no less passionate about the 'contests', and the desire for the hero to overcome the villain was as strong, if not stronger, than in any other group. Just as with literature or film, the ECW product showed that a compelling story can still hold the audience in is clutches.

ECW's fans had come to accept the contests weren't real, but they were so emotionally involved that it made no difference to their enjoyment.

The core of ECW was never the violence or the swearing or the adult themes. It was the simple philosophy of putting together the best show possible, by playing to strengths, hiding weaknesses, and never being afraid to try a new approach or change 'the rules' of the business. Tod Gordon and Paul Heyman's genius was nothing more complicated than building the product around the available talent instead of the other way round. They knew that manipulating an audience is not the same as conning it, and that the goal is not simply giving the fans what they want, but instead to make them want what you have to give them.

It is easy to understate the influence or success of Extreme Championship Wrestling. It was the third largest promotion in the United States of the past 15 years. Despite the woes of the final months, it gave many people a chance to make a decent living for several years. And it's effect on the business was not simply Steve Austin cursing and downing a beer. Those who point to the brawls of Memphis or the barbed wire of FMW as evidence that ECW created nothing original miss the point. ECW was about the ideal of acknowledging that the very fans who know how pro wrestling works are the ones who care the most passionately because they are *willingly* suspending disbelief. It was about understanding the difference between trying to make fans literally believe and giving them something believable. It was about having enough respect for an audience to see them as more than suckers to be scammed. Every time you see a performer give more than the bare minimum effort, or a promoter take a chance on something fresh and unproven you are, however indirectly, witnessing the influence of ECW.

The true business status of ECW is similarly misunderstood. On one hand the apologists produce a string of excuses, from the slow payment by pay-per-view firms to the limited promotion by TNN to the poor financial skills of Paul Heyman. On the other hand, the detractors paint a simple picture of a promotion with nothing more than a tiny cult audience incapable of drawing any serious money.

The reality of ECW's rise and fall is far simpler, and is not dependent on any one event. ECW had a sizeable audience (drawing nearly six million dollars in a year is not a cult business), but it operated in an era where that audience could not generate enough money to turn a profit, no matter how small or large ECW's operation was. Like every new promotion since the decline of the territories, ECW was dead the moment it ran its first show. Like any group that was started from scratch, it was inevitably headed for a vicious circle of necessary expansion and growth producing ever-deepening debts until reality hit. The need to clear debts could only be satisfied by increasing revenues, but with every attempt to do so, from pay-per-view to a busier schedule to national television, the associated costs grew at a quicker pace. Individual incidents and decisions might have hastened or lengthened this process, but the end result was as predetermined as any pro wrestling match.

ECW's fans have come to accept this reality. But we were so emotionally involved that it makes no difference to our memories.

Extreme Championship Wrestling could not live forever. Its legacy may never die.

Appendix: The ECW Alumni

The following is a complete listing of every person who wrestled a match for ECW, along with the date of their debut (in the UK day/month/year format). Performers are listed by the best-known ECW names, with other names they used in (parentheses). Names in [brackets] are those which they are best known by, but did not use in ECW.

The list includes a jointly promoted show with MEWF, but does not include two Japanese shows promoted under the IWA Japan banner.

If you find any mistakes, please send corrections to **corrections@turningthetables.co.uk**.

Jimmy Jannetty (25/2/92)
Steve Richards (25/2/92)
Super Destroyer (25/2/92)
Michael Bruno(25/2/92)
Tony Stetson (Broad Street Bully) (25/2/92)
Ivan Koloff(25/2/92)
Jeff Royal (25/2/92)
Max Thrasher (25/2/92)
Johnny Hotbody (25/2/92)
Larry Winters (25/2/92)
DC Drake (25/2/92)
JT Smith (25/2/92)
King Kaluha (24/3/92)
CN Redd (24/3/92)
Rick Perez (24/3/92)
Cry Baby Waldo (24/3/92)
Mr Anthony (24/3/92)
Glenn Osbourne (24/3/92)
Derrick Domino (24/3/92)
Super Destroyer II (24/3/92)

Salvatore Bellomo (Super Destroyer III) (25/4/92)
Jimmy Snuka (25/4/92)
Mr Perez (25/4/92)
Jim Curry (25/4/92)
Sandman (Mr Sandman) (25/4/92)
Pitbull 1 (25/4/92)
Pitbull 2 (25/4/92)
Metal Maniac (26/4/92)
HD Ryder (26/4/92)
John Rock (19/5/92)
The Anchor (19/5/92)
Chris Michaels (Richard Michaels) (19/5/92)
Vladmir Markoff (19/5/92)
Jim Neidhart (19/5/92)
Tatsumi Fujinami (26/5/92)
Chris Duffy (The Bouncer) (26/5/92)
Hurricane Curry (23/6/92)
Super Ninja (23/6/92)
Samoan Warrior (23/6/92)
Peaches (23/6/92)
Don E Allen (23/6/92)
Vivacious Veronica (23/6/92)
Don Muraco (23/6/92)
Stevie Wonderful (23/6/92)
Scott Summers (14/7/92)
Jack Hammer (14/7/92)
Tommy Cairo (14/7/92)
Little Guido (Damian Stone) (14/7/92)
Nikolai Volkoff (14/7/92)
Damian Knight (15/7/92)
Gino Caruso (12/8/92)
Hell Riders (12/8/92)
Soul Train Phillips (12/8/92)
EZ Ryder (22/8/92)
Fatu (12/9/92)
Rockin' Rebel (Mr X, Dark Ninja) (12/9/92)
Cream Team (12/9/92)

Rasta The Voodoo Mon (12/9/92)
Kodiak Bear (30/9/92)
Terry Taylor (30/9/92)
Rip Sawyer (3/10/92)
Dave Casanova (3/10/92)
Tigra (3/10/92)
Frank Cody (3/10/92)
Canadian Wolfman (3/10/92)
Renesta Benefica (16/11/92)
Davey Boy Smith (19/12/92)
Tod Gordon (19/12/92)
Hunter Q Robbins III (19/12/92)
Chris Evans (23/1/92)
Ray Odyssey (23/1/92)
Duane Gill (Lords of Darkness) (23/1/93)
Barry Hardy (Lords of Darkness) (23/1/93)
Kerry Von Erich (23/1/93)
Masked Superstar (23/1/93)
The Spider (23/1/93)
Terry Funk (23/1/93)
Eddie Gilbert (23/1/93)
Chris Candido (2/4/93)
Hawk (14/5/93)
Hinervo Rinestro (14/5/93)
Dick Murdoch (19/6/93)
Doug Gilbert (Dark Patriot II, Freddie Krueger) (19/6/93)
Headhunters (7/8/93)
Stan Hansen (7/8/93)
Masayoshi Motegi (7/8/93)
Miguel Perez Jr (7/8/93)
Mitushiro Matsunaga (7/8/93)
Tito Santana (8/8/93)
Rocco Rock (18/9/93)
Johnny Grunge (18/9/93)
Jason Knight (18/9/93)
Ian Rotten (18/9/93)
Kevin Sullivan (18/9/93)
Abdullah the Butcher (18/9/93)

Sherri Martel (18/9/93)
Jay Sulli (18/9/93)
Shane Douglas (18/9/93)
Crash the Terminator (18/9/93)
Axl Rotten (1/10/93)
Chad Austin (1/10/93)
Todd Shaw (1/10/93)
Silver Jet (1/10/93)
Malia Hosaka (1/10/93)
Holly McShane (1/10/93)
Paul Diamond (Max Moon) [Kato] (1/10/93)
Pat Tanaka (1/10/93)
Sabu (1/10/93)
Taz (Tazmaniac) (1/10/93)
Tommy Dreamer (2/10/93)
Johnny Gunn (22/10/93)
Mr Hughes (22/10/93)
Warlord (22/10/93)
Keith Scherer (12/11/93)
King Kong Bundy (13/11/93)
Watsumi the Rising Sun (14/11/93)
Joe College (14/11/93)
Johnny Paradise (14/11/93)
The Comet (14/11/93)
Pat Patterson Jr (14/11/93)
Colossal Kong (14/11/93)
Hack Myers (14/11/93)
Trent Young (14/11/93)
Mike Khoury (14/11/93)
Max Moon (14/11/93)
Tommy Lee Manson (14/11/93)
Bob Starr (14/11/93)
Junkyard Dog (14/11/93)
Southern Destruction (14/11/93)
Rich Myers (14/11/93)
Greg Valentine (14/11/93)
Lucifer the Knight of the Road (14/11/93)

Morgus the Maniac(14/11/93)
Jake Roberts (14/11/93)
Mike Norman (4/12/93)
The Lumberjack (4/12/93)
Mike Vee (4/12/93)
Mike Awesome (26/12/93)
Hollywood Kid (26/12/93)
Randy Starr (26/12/93)
Mikey Whipwreck (Mikey Wellbody) (8/1/94)
Frankenstein (8/1/94)
Dr Disaster (8/1/94)
Ron Harris (4/2/94)
Don Harris (4/2/94)
911 (5/2/94)
Paul Lauria (5/3/94)
Erik Anderson (6/3/94)
Billy Firehawk (6/3/94)
Judge Dread (6/3/94)
Devon Storm (6/3/94)
Young Dragons (6/3/94)
Billy Buster (26/3/94)
AJ Power (16/4/94)
Steve Collins (13/5/94)
Stan Parsons (13/5/94)
Woman (14/5/94)
Bobby Eaton (14/5/94)
Arn Anderson (14/5/94)
Dino Sendoff (Rolling Thunder) (3/6/94)
Joel Hartgood (3/6/94)
Too Cold Scorpio (3/6/94)
Dory Funk Jr (24/6/94)
Cactus Jack (24/6/94)
Bodyguard for Hire (26/5/94)
Phi Delta Slam (26/5/94)
Chris Benoit (27/8/94)
Matt Borne (27/8/94)
Dean Malenko (27/8/94)
Osamu Nishimura (27/8/94)

Chris Canyon (28/8/94)
Penny Pulsations (20/9/94)
Ron Simmons (15/10/94)
Jim Powers (4/11/94)
Joe Malenko (19/11/94)
Chaos (16/11/94)
Tully Blanchard (7/1/95)
Kendal Windham (14/1/95)
Mr President (14/1/95)
Death Row (14/1/95)
Horace Hogan (Prey of the Dead) (16/1/95)
Jason the Terrible (4/2/95)
Hector Guerrero (24/2/95)
Marty Jannetty (25/2/95)
Raven (17/3/95)
Eddy Guerrero (8/4/95)
Tsubo Genjin (15/4/95)
Alex G (5/5/95)
The Evil Snake (5/5/95)
Norman Smiley (5/5/95)
Miguel San Juan (6/5/95)
Hiroyoshi Ikuda (13/5/95)
Doug Flex (20/5/95)
New Jersey Devil [Doug Gentry of RF Video] (17/6/95)
Vampire Warrior (17/6/95)
Jim Steele (Wolf Hawkfield) (17/6/95)
Beulah McGillicutty (17/6/95)
Luna Vachon (17/6/95)
Dudley Dudley (1/7/95)
Little Snot Dudley (1/7/95)
Val Puccio (Big Malley, Big Valley) (1/7/95)
New Jack (1/7/95)
Mustafa Saed (1/7/95)
Bull Pain (20/7/95)
Joe DiFuria (Purple Haze) (20/7/95)
Demon Hellstorm (20/7/95)
David Sierra (The Terrorist, Fidel Sierra, Mr Puerto Rico)

(20/7/95)

    Primo Carnera III (28/7/95)
    Rick Steiner (28/7/95)
    Scott Steiner (28/7/95)
    Francine (26/8/95)
    Dances With Dudley (28/8/95)
    Perry Saturn (17/9/95)
    John Kronus (17/9/95)
    Rey Misterio Jr (17/9/95)
    Psicosis (17/9/95)
    Konnan (6/10/95)
    Pablo Pena (7/10/95)
    Big Dick Dudley (7/10/95)
    Buh Buh Ray Dudley (27/10/95)
    El Puerto Ricano (Pablo Marquez) (28/10/95)
    La Parka (28/10/95)
    Bad Crew (3/11/95)
    Flamingo Kid (3/11/95)
    Ranger Seven (17/11/95)
    George Love (17/11/95)
    Bill Alfonso (18/11/95)
    Steve Austin (18/11/95)
    Sweet Georgia Brown (1/12/95)
    Blue Meanie (1/12/95)
    Bruiser Mastino [Mantaur] (1/12/95)
    Jimmy Del Ray (9/12/95)
    Tom Prichard (9/12/95)
    Koji Nakagawa (28/12/95)
    Rob Van Dam (6/1/96)
    Dreg (27/1/96)
    Shark Attack Kid (2/2/96)
    Chris Jericho (2/2/96)
    Juventud Guerrera (3/2/96)
    Dirtbike Kid (17/2/96)
    Spiros Greco (17/2/96)
    Bam Bam Bigelow (23/2/96)
    Big Titan (8/3/96)
    Chubby Dudley (15/3/96)

Damian Kane (30/3/96)
Dark Riders (30/3/96)
Billy Black (12/4/96)
Damien 666 (13/4/96)
Super Nova (20/4/96)
Brian Lee (20/4/96)
Beef Wellington (11/5/96)
Italian Stallions (18/5/96)
Slice & Dice Ramirez (18/5/96)
Jason Helton (1/6/96)
Terry Gordy (22/6/96)
Samoan Gangsta Party (22/6/96)
Louie Spicolli (12/7/96)
Havoc Inc (12/7/96)
Tarzan Goto (12/7/96)
Big Guido (13/7/96)
Johnny Smith (2/8/96)
Steve Williams (3/8/96)
Doug Furnas (24/8/96)
Dan Kroffat (14/9/96)
Jim Callusio (27/9/96)
Exotic Experience (27/9/96)
Spike Dudley (1/10/96)
Cody Michaels (26/10/96)
Kid Kash (Davey Morton Tyler Jericho, Davey Paisano) (2/11/96)
Gorgeous Quatermain (29/11/96)
Rick Rage (7/12/96)
Gary Albright (7/12/96)
Balls Mahoney (20/12/96)
Jimmy Cicero (28/12/96)
Chris Van De Lay (3/1/97)
Tommy Rich (11/1/97)
Ricky Morton (11/1/97)
Roadkill (31/1/97)
Chris Chetti (31/1/97)
Scott Taylor [Scotty 2 Hotty] (14/2/97)

Lenny Lane (14/2/97)
Dick Togo (14/2/97)
Terry Boy (14/2/97)
Taka Michinoku (14/2/97)
Gran Naniwa (14/2/97)
Great Sasuke (14/2/97)
Gran Hamada (14/2/97)
Bobby Duncum Jr (14/2/97)
Tracey Smothers (22/2/97)
Corporal Punishment (1/3/97)
Lance Storm (1/3/97)
Lost Boys (28/3/97)
Masato Yakushiji (13/4/97)
Wild Bill (Boogaloo Bill) (25/4/97)
Wing Kanemura (Kintaro Kanemura) (2/5/97)
Kevin Quinn (2/5/97)
Bill Willcox (2/5/97)
Jamie Dundee (10/5/97)
Wolfie D (10/5/97)
Danny Doring (Danny Morrison) (20/6/97)
Bud Licious (11/7/97)
Jimmy Shoulders (11/7/97)
Hellraiser (12/7/97)
Tom Marquez (The Prodigy, El Diablo) (19/7/97)
Jerry Lawler (19/7/97)
Rick Rude (19/7/97)
Marty Barnett (25/7/97)
Lou Marconi (1/8/97)
Los Cholos (1/8/97)
Justin Credible (PG 187, PJ Walker) (21/8/97)
Jerry Lynn (6/9/97)
Bill Wyles (Bilvis Wesley) (6/9/97)
Bob Watson (3/10/97)
Tommy Rogers (30/10/97)
Erin O'Grady [Crash Holly] (7/11/97)
Chastity (20/11/97)
Tiger Mask IV (26/12/97)
Adam Flash (27/12/97)

Brackus (9/1/98)
Mike Anthony (16/1/98)
Darren Drozdov (20/2/98)
Masato Tanaka (1/3/98)
Ulf Herman (20/3/98)
Bushwhackers (9/4/98)
Sam Fatu (9/4/98)
Mike Lozansky (15/5/98)
Equalizer (20/6/98)
Atsushi Onita (27/6/98)
Michael Kovacs (10/7/98)
Jinsei Shinzaki [Hakushi] (2/8/98)
Hayabusa (2/8/98)
Dr Luther (14/9/98)
Sal E Graziano (20/8/98)
Rod Price (3/9/98)
One Man Gang (5/9/98)
Kevin Northcutt (4/10/98)
Chris Walker (4/10/98)
Sammy Solo (4/10/98)
Robert Gibson (15/10/98)
Rex King (16/10/98)
Mabel [Viscera] (Not in a scheduled match, but was pinned by Spike Dudley during a Tracey Smothers vs Tommy Rogers match) (1/11/98)
Skull Von Krush (14/11/98)
Spanish Angel (5/12/98)
Antifaz del Norte (19/12/98)
Yoshihiro Tajiri (19/12/98)
Steve Corino (19/12/98)
Super Crazy (26/12/98)
Sid (10/1/99)
Mosco de la Merced (1/4/99)
Papi Chulo [Essa Rios] (3/4/99)
Rhino (Rhino Richards) (10/4/99)
Ricky Santana (29/4/99)
Tony DeVito (7/5/99)

Simon Diamond (Lance Diamond) (7/5/99)
Steve Nixon (20/5/99)
CW Anderson (11/6/99)
Christopher Daniels (17/6/99)
Horace the Psychopath (17/6/99)
Tom Morgan (17/6/99)
Jazz (8/7/99)
Vito Legrasso (8/7/99)
Super Leather [Corporal Kirschner] (9/7/99)
Bubba The Love Sponge (10/7/99)
Kimala II (Uganda) (31/7/99)
PN News (28/8/99)
Jesus Christobol (11/9/99)
Miss Congeniality [Lita] (23/9/99)
Mad Dog Kimble (26/9/99)
Chad (26/9/99)
Bo Dupp (30/9/99)
Jack Dupp (30/9/99)
Pump Dupp (Cham Pain) (30/9/99)
Musketeer (16/10/99)
HC Loc (16/10/99)
Worton, Scott (29/10/99)
Dick Hertz (11/11/99)
Super Calo (2/12/99)
Vic Grimes (10/12/99)
Erik Watts (15/1/00)
Ricky Banderas (22/1/00)
Josh Wilcox(22/1/00)
Julio Dinero (Julio Fantastico) (22/1/00)
Scott D'Amore (25/2/00)
Chilly Willy (25/2/00)
Gedo (4/3/00)
Jado (4/3/00)
Johnny Swinger (24/3/00)
Mad Dog Mike (28/4/00)
Scott Anton [Scotty Riggs] (29/4/00)
Bill Irwin (5/5/00)
Chris Hamrick (20/5/00)

Jorge Estrada (26/5/00)
Tony Mamaluke (26/5/00)
Shawn Evans (27/5/00)
Prime Time (27/5/00)
Steve Skyfire (2/6/00)
Chaz Taylor (3/6/00)
Jean Pierre LaFitte (10/6/00)
EZ Money (10/6/00)
Nick Bell [Mike Bell] (16/6/00)
Red Dog [Rodney Mack] (30/6/00)
Willy Frazier (21/7/00)
Michael Shane (4/8/00)
Chris Cruger (11/8/00)
Oz (11/8/00)
Christian York (20/8/00)
Joey Matthews [Joey Mercury of MNM] (20/8/00)
Prodigette (22/9/00)
Blacksmith (22/9/00)
Lou E Dangerously (22/9/00)
Danny Daniels (22/9/00)
Joel Gertner (7/10/00)
Cyrus (7/10/00)
Scott Hall (10/11/00)
Phoenix (12/1/01)

By the same author

Slamthology
343 Pages
ISBN: 1-905290-10-1

John Lister is one of Britain's most respected wrestling journalists. Mixing travelogue, humour, fiction, history and opinion, *Slamthology* brings together the best of his work from the past fourteen years.

The first section of this book features three epic accounts of voyages to see wrestling in the United States, from the ECW Arena to the Dallas Sportatorium by way of WWF pay-per-views and Memphis television.

The second section comprises more than 40 articles, some previously unpublished, including histories of British and American wrestling, the statistics behind WCW's collapse, and a disgraceful allegation about Tommy Rich.

For full details, or to order your copy, please visit **www.slamthology.co.uk**

Printed in the United Kingdom
by Lightning Source UK Ltd.
120757UK00002B/232-234